_10-18_

Dante Gabriel Rossetti's
Versecraft

Joseph F. Vogel

University of Florida Press

Gainesville • 1971

COPYRIGHT © 1971 BY THE STATE OF FLORIDA
DEPARTMENT OF GENERAL SERVICES

LIBRARY OF CONGRESS
CATALOG CARD No. 76-150655
ISBN 0-8130-0324-5

PRINTED BY THE STORTER PRINTING COMPANY
GAINESVILLE, FLORIDA

Acknowledgments

Every author of a critical study owes a debt to those who have helped to prepare him. My own debt is greatest to Professors Clark Emery of the University of Miami, Thomas Pyles of Northwestern University, and T. Walter Herbert and Ants Oras of the University of Florida. To Professor Oras especially, who first interested me in prosody and in Rossetti, and whose advice and criticism have been invaluable to the present study, I am most grateful. Finally, for her patience with me and her impatience with unclear sentences, I wish to thank my wife, Phyllis.

Contents

Introduction   1

1. Meter   6

2. Stanzaic Forms—Structure and Rhythm   41

3. Rhyme and Other Sound Echoing   71

4. "The Blessed Damozel"   91

Introduction

Every art is partly a craft, and in poetry the craft is versification. The importance of versification, although never denied, is seldom fully appreciated. It is obvious to anybody that a substantial change in the subject matter of *Lycidas,* for example, would result in a different poem. But if substantially the same subject matter had been shaped into rhymed couplets or ottava rima the poem would also be very different, if it managed to remain a poem at all, and this latter fact is obvious to relatively few people. The ordinary reader knows little more about versification than the standard meters and verse forms described in handbooks of prosody. And this is not necessarily deplorable, since the rhythms and sounds will affect him anyway, if he really hears the poetry (though the more he knows about versification, the more acutely he tends to hear). But it is otherwise for the critic, whose business is not simply to enjoy poetry but to perceive how it works to produce enjoyment. He needs to know such things as the subtly different ways in which different poets may handle the same meters and verse forms, the devices of sound, syntax, and structure that are peculiar to particular poets, and the manner in which such traits affect the poetry. It is techniques and traits of this kind, as they appear in the poetry of Dante Gabriel Rossetti, that are the subject of the present study.

Nothing like a thorough study of prosody has been given to any but a handful of major poets. Since major poets tend to be excellent craftsmen, they deserve such attention. But it does not follow that a poet of less stature like Rossetti might not have been a superior craftsman also. (One thinks of Browning's Andrea del Sarto, incapable of great painting but capable of giving Raphael lessons in technique.) For Rossetti, though a painter by profession, was anything but an amateur as a poet. In fact, he seems to have been more dili-

1

gent in learning to write verse than in learning to paint. In youth his distaste for instruction in fundamentals of technique brought on problems in painting that reduced him to throwing himself down and howling.[1] But he studied versification eagerly from childhood, writing metrically correct blank verse at the precocious age of six[2] and producing at thirteen a poem in which he experimented successfully with several different meters.[3] He learned, of course, by studying the poets, and his excuse when he shocked his aunt by reading the "atheistical" Shelley—that he did so "solely on account of the splendid versification"[4]—was undoubtedly the truth, if perhaps not the whole truth. At sixteen he had the skill to translate Burger's *Lenore* into accomplished verse.[5] By nineteen he had written "The Blessed Damozel," and though he later polished a few details of its meter, even the first version of that poem is a superb example of prosodic art.

Rossetti was not only skillful but painstaking—a most romantic poet, yet the very opposite of the romantic stereotype dashing off the finished products of his inspiration. He spoke unromantically of writing poetry as "fundamental brainwork";[6] and he was, his brother William Rossetti said, "a very fastidious writer" who "abhorred anything straggling, slipshod, profuse, or uncondensed" and who often recurred to his old poems to perfect them.[7] Although versification was not the only concern of this perfectionism, it was an important part of it; many of Rossetti's emendations were prosodic, and when he asked for an opinion about his work, usually from his brother but sometimes from Swinburne or William Allingham, the matter was more often than not a question of meter or sound. All this prosodic study and care, Rossetti himself believed, eventually made him an accomplished craftsman—and he was neither vain nor easily satisfied. For he was certainly not belittling the skill he had acquired as a mature and distinguished painter when he said, according to his

1. Oswald Doughty, *A Victorian Romantic: Dante Gabriel Rossetti* (London, 1960), p. 77.
2. *Dante Gabriel Rossetti: His Family-Letters,* ed. William M. Rossetti (Boston, 1895), I, 65.
3. Ibid., I, 84.
4. Ibid., II, 19.
5. *The Works of Dante Gabriel Rossetti,* ed. William M. Rossetti (London, 1911), p. 678, n. to p. 501.
6. T. Hall Caine, *Recollections of Dante Gabriel Rossetti* (Boston, 1898), p. 249.
7. *Works,* p. xx.

brother, that "he thought he had mastered the means of embodying poetical conceptions in the verbal and rhythmical vehicle more thoroughly than in form and design, perhaps more thoroughly than in color."[8]

Rossetti's versification has received considerable praise but little analysis. The most important general studies of the poetry, by A. C. Benson[9] and by R. L. Megroz,[10] and some shorter articles, contain occasional remarks about the versification. George Saintsbury's treatment of Rossetti in *A History of English Prosody* calls attention to a few meters and stanzas, usually with admiration but with no attempt to analyze the causes of the admired effects.[11] In his edition of "The House of Life," Paull Franklin Baum summarizes some traits of Rossetti's sonnet rhymes and structures,[12] and in his edition of "The Blessed Damozel" he offers useful comments about the poem's versification.[13] That poem is the only one whose meter has been analyzed thoroughly, though not quite validly, in a study by Elizabeth Jackson,[14] whose main conclusion I shall show cause to disagree with. Even if all the above treatments were entirely adequate there would be much more to say, because Rossetti's versification varies too greatly in different poems to be completely characterized by the few poems that critics have touched upon.

The present study, then, treats more of the poetry and analyzes it more closely than has yet been done. In three main areas of prosody—meter, verse structures such as sonnets and stanzas, and rhyme and other sounds—it summarizes Rossetti's main general traits. Then, and most importantly, it describes as many as could be discovered of his special techniques, his tricks of the prosodic trade, which go beyond the elementary practices used to produce conventional verse. It has been unnecessary to discuss all the poems individually; many, like the sonnets, are homogeneous enough to be considered usually as a group and some others exhibit no traits that could not be described in connection with other poems. Partly for

8. Ibid., p. xxi.
9. *Rossetti* (New York, 1911).
10. *Dante Gabriel Rossetti: Painter Poet of Heaven and Earth* (New York, 1929).
11. London, 1910, III, 310–16.
12. Cambridge, Mass., 1928.
13. *The Blessed Damozel: The Unpublished Manuscript Texts and Collation* (Chapel Hill, 1937).
14. "Notes on the Stanza of Rossetti's 'The Blessed Damozel,'" *PMLA*, 58 (Dec., 1943), 1050–56.

this last reason the translations are not discussed, nor are poems left unpublished by Rossetti except for a few references to juvenile ballads. The second reason for this exclusion is that it seems invalid to base an idea of his craftsmanship on verse that he regarded as metrically flawed, as he admitted was the case with some translations[15] and as may have been the case with poems withheld until after his death.

Many of the findings I shall present are based on statistics—a counting of the frequency of various traits of verse. To literary critics, much concerned with aesthetics, such an unemotional procedure may seem uncongenial. But statistics are indispensable for verifying or invalidating one's subjective impressions about prosodic traits. Furthermore they may reveal traits that might otherwise have gone unnoticed because those traits do not normally impinge on a reader's conscious attention. However, I have tried to present statistics unobtrusively and only as evidence for stated conclusions, not as a source from which the reader must deduce conclusions. In one area, scansion, statistics are certainly questionable—which leads me to the prosodist's customary acknowledgment of fallibility: although I have sought to make my scansion as normal as possible, others might sometimes disagree with it. But that fact is less invalidating than might seem, because the scansion is only a preliminary basis for a further comparison—between, for example, the meters of Rossetti and Keats. And while someone might differ with me about the exact number of irregular feet used by each poet, we would almost surely agree about the more important question of which poet used the larger number.

In its main purpose this study is different from some other prosodic analyses. These have investigated a poet's traits of versification per se to establish a description of his practice, with perhaps the further aim of showing whom he influenced or was influenced by, or of exhibiting chronological changes in his style. They have not been mainly concerned with the question of what difference the traits make in the poetry. That question is central in the present study. After discovering a prosodic trait, I have tried to determine what is achieved by it—the manner in which it interacts with the subject matter to help create the total effect of the poetry. Such matters as influences and chronological development are noted

15. Rossetti commented on unavoidable prosodic imperfections in his translations in *Dante and His Circle* (London, 1874), pp. ix–x.

when they are pertinent, but they have not been a main concern.

Nor does this study have a particular case to argue; it is almost entirely an exposition of Rossetti's methods. But it does, I believe, tend to prove one thing by implication—that Rossetti was a remarkably fine craftsman. One critic, Ford Madox Ford, thought otherwise, declaring that Swinburne was a poet "far excelling Rossetti in the technique of verse-making."[16] But the evidence from Rossetti's poetry (Ford offers no evidence at all) suggests that such an opinion could be held only by a critic too much impressed by Swinburne's obvious virtuosity in meter and sound and too little observant of the more subtle techniques of Rossetti.

The first three chapters which follow deal respectively with meter, stanzas and other verse forms, and sound. Some poems are of interest for more than one of those elements, and it has generally been convenient to recur to those poems in each of the relevant chapters. But the analysis of meter and stanza in "The Blessed Damozel," being longer and more detailed, is presented as a unit in a separate concluding chapter.

16. Ford Madox Hueffer, *Rossetti: A Critical Essay on His Art* (London, 1902), p. 43.

1

Meter

In Rossetti's era the modern trend toward a freer prosody was already active in the experimental rhythms of poets like Whitman, Hopkins, Meredith, and Henley. But Rossetti himself was no revolutionary, nor did he aspire to be one. "After the first experimental years of youth were past," his brother wrote, "he was opposed to innovations in rhythm and metre; thinking that the established and recognized forms are generally the best."[1] In fact, if any of his youthful verse was radically unconventional he must have discarded it, for despite the metrical variety of the extant poems none of them depart altogether from traditional meters.

And even within traditional meters Rossetti was conservative in some ways, employing mostly iambic in the more common line lengths. He used no meters as strikingly unusual as the trochaic octameter of Tennyson's "Locksley Hall" or the anapestic hexameter of Swinburne's "Hymn to Proserpine." He avoided triple meter (although he sometimes used triple feet freely as a variation in duple meter) except when he turned to dactylic tetrameter to get a special musical effect in "Song of the Bower" and when he wrote "Sacrament Hymn" in anapestic meter "merely to see if I could do Wesley."[2] And he used trochaic only for a few short lyrics and, in a highly varied form, for the ballads "Troy Town" and "Eden Bower." All the rest of the verse is iambic: nearly one-fourth of this is the iambic pentameter of the sonnets and of the blank verse monologue "A Last Confession"; another fourth is the more irregular iambic of the ballads; most of the remainder is the iambic tetrameter of various narratives, monologues, and lyrics; and a few short lyrics are in iambic trimeter.

Rossetti certainly did not adhere to standard meters merely out of regard for convention, any more than he would have abandoned them merely to be different. His reason, one feels after studying

1. *Works*, p. 659, n. to p. 114.
2. Ibid., p. 666, n. to p. 192.

his methods, must have been his conviction that the best means of poetic expression are those standard meters, skillfully varied in ways appropriate to the subject matter. By using such variations with originality and boldness he created a highly individual and effective metrical style. Individuality is easy for a poet who invents his own meter—indeed it is automatic; but it is more difficult for one who confines himself to common meters and their accepted variations. And when one perceives the manner in which Rossetti achieved this individuality, one is enlightened about the capacities and nuances of these meters.

A common way of exhibiting a poet's metrical skill is to offer examples of "imitative" meter—lines in which the rhythm strikingly accords with the sense, like Pope's famous alexandrine "That, like a wounded snake, drags its slow length along." Rossetti's verse contains numerous imitative lines. For example, when he described a girl in "Jenny" his poet's ear helped to emphasize details visualized by his painter's eye:

> As Jén/ny's lóng / thróat dróops / asíde,—
> The shád/ows where / the chéeks / are thín,
> The púre / wíde cúrve / from eár / to chín.[3]

The weight added to the tetrameter meter by spondees in the first and third lines accentuates the length of Jenny's throat and the wide curve of her jaw, while the lightening of the second line by a pyrrhic, resulting in only three stressed syllables, accords with the thinness of her cheeks.[4]

3. Except where otherwise specified, the *Works* of 1911 has been used as the source of all quotations and the basis of all analysis of Rossetti's poetry.

4. In scansion I use the traditional method of marking syllables according to stress and dividing lines into metrical feet to exhibit the predominant standard meter. Presumably Rossetti based his verse on standard meters; certainly all of his verse corresponds closely enough to one or another of those meters so that it can be scanned in this way. And this method, besides indicating how the verse is read, reveals the metrical peculiarities of the verse by showing how it deviates from an ideally regular form of the standard meter. The result makes possible a comparison between different examples of verse based on that meter. I have scanned all the verse according to four levels of stress. But except where reference to four levels is necessary to show certain traits of meter, I shall for simplicity refer to or exhibit only two levels—"stressed," meaning primary (´) and secondary (ʌ) stress, and "unstressed," meaning tertiary (ꙮ) and weak (‿) stress.

A more extended example of imitative meter occurs in "The Card Dealer," a poem written in ballad stanzas extended to six lines, with conventional iambic meter except for a number of substituted anapests—ten in fifty-four lines. What is striking is that all ten anapests are used imitatively. One of them gives a rhythmic lilt to a line about music:

> *As a tune* / within / a tune.

Another anapest suggests the liveliness of play in

> With thee / *it is play*/ing still.

And a third accentuates the swaying motion in

> Beneath / the sway / *o' the sun.*

The remaining anapests are crowded into a single one of the poem's nine stanzas, a stanza that paraphrases a verse in Job (10:22) about the absence of order in the world of death. That theme of disorder Rossetti emphasizes by an accompanying metrical disorder, produced by the abrupt plethora of anapests together with a terminal pyrrhic in the fourth line and two inverted feet that make the meter crumble in the last half of the first line:

> A land / without / any / order,—
> Day ev/*en as night,* / (one saith,)—
> *Where who li*/eth down / aris/eth not
> *Nor the sleep*/*er awak*/eneth;
> A land / of dark/*ness as dark*/*ness itself*
> And of / the shad/*ow of death.*

Many other examples of Rossetti's imitative meter can be found, but the value of exhibiting them here is limited. True, imitative lines show a poet's cleverness in making sound reinforce sense. But they do not adequately characterize his meter, because they constitute by far the smaller part of any poet's verse. The reason is that ideas can be imitated by analogous qualities of meter only if they contain connotations such as movement, weight, or duration; but only a minority of the ideas in poetry are of this kind. Is the remainder of the verse, then, the nonimitative majority of the lines, no more than an inert background for occasional imitative lines? Quite the contrary: that remainder is the main metrical source of emotion in the poetry, simply because it does constitute the larger part of the verse and affects the reader continuously if unconsciously, in different ways according to its varying qualities.

Consequently, while I shall note imitative effects when they are encountered, my main purpose will be to describe those more general and pervasive qualities of Rossetti's meter and to appraise their effects. This can be done most conveniently by examining two main classes of meter—the more conventional iambic used in most of the poems and best represented by the sonnets, and the more irregular meter (one might say "meters" because of their variety) of the ballads and certain poems related to them.

SONNET METER

In order to discover the metrical traits of Rossetti's sonnets I have scanned eighty of them. These have been divided into four groups of twenty each, chosen to reveal any chronological development in style: Group I, written before 1855; Group II, written between 1867 (when Rossetti resumed writing after an unproductive period following his wife's death in 1862) and the publication of the *Poems* of 1870; Group III, written during a prolific period from 1870 to 1873; and Group IV, written between 1874 and Rossetti's death in 1882. And in order to discover in what ways, if any, Rossetti's metrical traits are different from those of other poets, I have scanned the eighteen sonnets of Milton and a group of twenty sonnets of Keats and have compared them with Rossetti's in various ways. Thus the statistics and tables below which exhibit these comparisons refer to six groups of sonnets: Milton's, Keats's, and four groups of Rossetti's.[5]

The differences between a poet's methods and the methods of other poets may seem more interesting than the similarities, but

5. Except for the chronological requirement, which made it necessary to include some of his miscellaneous sonnets to complete Groups I and IV, Rossetti's sonnets were chosen at random from those of "The House of Life." Keats's, chosen at random from those having, like Rossetti's, the Italian rhyme scheme, were taken from *The Poetical Works of John Keats,* ed. H. W. Garrod (London, 1956), and Milton's from *The Works of John Milton,* eds. Frank Patterson et al. (New York, 1931).

the similarities also help to characterize his style. In his use of certain metrical devices Rossetti's practice differs little from that of Milton or Keats. One of these devices is the substitution of inverted feet, or trochees, for iambs. The average number per sonnet used by both Milton (4.1) and Keats (3.9) is larger, but only slightly, than the number used by Rossetti in his four groups (I–3.6, II–3.2, III–3.1, IV–3.1), and Rossetti's use did not change significantly during his career. It is worth observing, however, that the actual number of inverted feet in particular sonnets of all three poets sometimes varies considerably from the average, with Milton using as few as one and as many as six, Keats as few as one and as many as eight, and Rossetti as few as none and as many as nine.

Inverted feet are a common variation in poetry, of course, occurring usually in the first position of the line, where Milton and Keats place about 80 per cent of theirs. This gives the line an arresting beginning that may lend considerable rhetorical force to sonnets having several such lines. Rossetti places fewer (65 per cent) of his inversions in the initial position; nevertheless he writes more lines with strong beginnings than Milton and Keats because of his more frequent use of initial spondees. Rossetti's tendency to place more (35 per cent) of his inversions within the line hardly affects his meter much, since that amount constitutes an average of only one medial inversion per sonnet. It is indicative, however, of his more general tendency to use a less orthodox, more irregular meter than Milton or Keats.

In using anapests as a variation in iambic meter there is again no great difference among the three poets. Rossetti's earliest sonnets average slightly fewer (.6 anapests per sonnet) than those of Milton (1.6) and Keats (1.1), and his, like theirs, are nearly all elidible. In his later groups he averages a few more (II–3.1, III–3.4, IV–3.5), although not more than are sometimes used in particular sonnets by Milton (4) and Keats (5). The largest number in a sonnet of Rossetti's is seven. But since an average of only one anapest per sonnet in these later groups is unelidible, they affect the meter only slightly. Rossetti could be extraordinarily free with anapests in some poetry, especially ballads, but he used them with restraint in such a formal genre as the sonnet.

Caesuras are partly an aspect of a rhythmic movement which is larger than meter—that produced by the way syntax is arranged into lines, stanzas, and other verse units—and they will be referred to in the chapter on that subject. But they also affect the metrical movement within lines. Here again Rossetti's practice is fairly close to that of Milton and Keats. His sonnets average slightly fewer punctuated pauses within lines (6.92 per sonnet) than Milton's (7.98) and Keats's (7.75), and slightly fewer of his pauses are full stops. All three poets punctuate most often after the fourth, sixth, and fifth syllables, in that order of frequency, but Rossetti is somewhat more prone to punctuate at the less conventional positions nearer the beginning and end of lines. In general, then, his sonnets tend to have a smoother, less frequently interrupted movement of syntax than theirs; and more of his pauses produce a dramatic effect because of their asymmetrical position. But these differences in his practice are slight.

———————

So far, then, Rossetti's meter exhibits about the same kind and amount of variations as that of the other two poets. But differences appear—differences that constitute distinctive Rossettian traits— when one studies the number of stressed and unstressed syllables in the sonnets of the several groups. To explain: suppose one were to write a perfectly regular sonnet (a difficult and undesirable thing to do). It would contain 140 syllables, 70 unstressed and 70 stressed, arranged in 70 iambs. Now if one introduced a spondee in place of an iamb, there would be 71 stressed syllables and 69 unstressed syllables—every spondee adds one stressed syllable and subtracts one unstressed syllable. On the other hand, if one had introduced a pyrrhic in place of an iamb, there would have been 69 stressed syllables and 71 unstressed syllables—every pyrrhic subtracts one stressed syllable and adds one unstressed syllable. Thus sonnets vary from the hypothetical balance of 70 unstressed and 70 stressed syllables according to their number of pyrrhics and spondees. (An unelidible anapest adds one unstressed syllable without changing the number of stressed syllables, but there are so few in the sonnets being studied that they can be safely disregarded.)

Milton's sonnets average 71.8 stressed syllables (68.2 unstressed) —somewhat more than the number in a regular sonnet. Keats's sonnets tend to be lighter in stress, averaging only 68.3 stressed syllables (71.7 unstressed). Rossetti's tend to be heavier than theirs: his earliest group averages 72.1 stressed syllables, slightly more than Milton's and significantly more than Keats's; and this tendency toward heaviness increases in the later sonnets, with an average of

74 stressed syllables in Group II, 74.8 in Group III, and 74.3 in Group IV.

Perhaps these differences may seem less important than they are—the difference, for example, of an average of two or three stressed syllables between Milton's sonnets and most of Rossetti's. But it should be remembered that when three stressed syllables are added to a sonnet, three unstressed syllables that might have occupied those positions are eliminated and their lightening effect is dispensed with. The case is not like adding weight to one end of a scale balance with the weight at the other end remaining the same; it is like transferring weight from one end to the other. So the actual difference in the weight of stress produced by a difference of three stressed syllables is twice what that number suggests. This does make the difference between Milton's and Rossetti's sonnets important; and between Keats's and Rossetti's the difference, about six stressed syllables, is even more important. It is a difference in the feel of the meter and, since stressed syllables produce forceful utterance, a difference in the rhetorical impact.

But it would be misleading to suggest that all of Rossetti's sonnets are stronger in stress than all of Milton's and Keats's. Again the variations of particular sonnets from the average are wide. Five of Milton's contain more stressed syllables (as many as 81, in "To the Nightingale") than Rossetti's average, and so does one of Keats's (76, in "To Chatterton"). And though several of Rossetti's contain more than 80 stressed syllables (as many as 87, in Sonnet XIII of "The House of Life"), some are lighter in stress than most of Keats's and one (the "Introductory Sonnet," with 61) is lighter than any sonnet of the other two poets. It can be said, then, that more of his sonnets than of theirs are heavy in stress, and that he shows a wide variation from the average, usually toward heaviness but sometimes toward lightness.

The question of why Rossetti's sonnets tend to be heavy in stress leads to the discovery of traits of style which, though not strictly metrical, are worth observing. One answer that suggests itself is monosyllabity. That is, one-syllable words may or may not be stressed, but words of two or more syllables, with rare exceptions, contain some syllables that must be unstressed. If, instead of a three-syllable word in which only one syllable can be stressed, a poet uses three one-syllable words, perhaps two or three of the latter might be stressed. Consequently it would seem that a higher percentage of monosyllabity would result in a larger proportion of stressed syllables.

This hypothesis is supported to some extent by the table below, which shows for comparison the average number of stressed syllables per sonnet together with the percentage of monosyllabic words for each of the groups:

	Stressed Syllables	Monosyllabic Words (in percentages)
M.	71.8	79.6
K.	68.3	75
R.—I	72.1	82.8
II	74	81
III	74.8	80.5
IV	74.3	77.5

Keats's sonnets contain the fewest stressed syllables and are the least monosyllabic. Milton uses more stressed syllables than Keats and is more monosyllabic. Rossetti uses still more stressed syllables and is more monosyllabic than Milton in three of his groups. Also, in individual sonnets differences in the number of stressed syllables tend to be accompanied by corresponding differences in monosyllabity: for example, Rossetti's Sonnet XIII contains 87 stressed syllables and is 86 per cent monosyllabic, whereas the "Introductory Sonnet" contains only 61 stressed syllables and is only 72 per cent monosyllabic. However, there are some differences that the hypothesis does not account for. Rossetti's three later groups, being less monosyllabic than his earliest, might be expected to have fewer stressed syllables, but they have more. And some individual sonnets that are equally monosyllabic show a difference of several stressed syllables. Apparently monosyllabity does tend to increase the number of stressed syllables, but it cannot be the only factor.

A fuller explanation for the differences in the number of stressed syllables is revealed when one analyzes the kinds of words used by the three poets. Words can be divided into three classes with regard to metrical stress. One class consists of articles and the shorter and more common prepositions and conjunctions; these are metrically weak words that are nearly always unstressed, even when they occur in positions of normal metrical stress. A second class consists of most auxiliary verbs, copulas, pronouns, and some prepositions and conjunctions; these, which might be called metrically neutral, are usually stressed when they occur in positions of metrical stress and unstressed when they occur in the unstressed positions. The third class consists of metrically strong words—nouns and gerunds, verbs and verbal participles, adjectives and adjectival participles, adverbs, and interjections; these words, or at least their accented syllable when they contain more than one syllable, will nearly always be stressed even in normally unstressed positions of the meter. This trait of strong words is illustrated in the following line, in which stress is given not only to the words in positions of normal metrical stress but also to three strong words in normally unstressed positions—the noun in the third position, the interjection in the fifth position, and the adjective in the ninth position:

When that / mist cleared, / Ó Shel/ley! what / dread veil.

Presumably, then, a high proportion of strong words will produce a high proportion of stressed syllables. This is largely borne out by the following table, which shows the average number of stressed syllables and strong words per sonnet used by the three poets:

	Stressed Syllables	Strong Words
M.	71.8	64.8
K.	68.3	63.1
R.—I	72.1	63.8
II	74	65.9
III	74.8	68.3
IV	74.3	68.5

With one exception, every group that averages as many as one stressed syllable more than another group also averages more strong words. In some cases the correspondence is close: Rossetti's Groups III and IV average about six more stressed syllables and five more strong words than Keats's, and about three more stressed syllables and three more strong words than Milton's. Where the correspondence is less close, or where there is no correspondence, the main cause is probably monosyllabity, which permits the inclusion of, in addition to strong words, more neutral words that fall in positions where they receive stress. Thus, in the exception just mentioned,

Rossetti's Group I averages slightly fewer strong words than Milton's group and about the same number as Keats's; yet it averages slightly more stressed syllables than Milton's and almost four more than Keats's—but Rossetti's group is 3 per cent more monosyllabic than Milton's and nearly 6 per cent more monosyllabic than Keats's. Another discrepancy is that Rossetti's Groups III and IV average two to three more strong words than Group II without producing any significant increase in the number of stressed syllables; here the reason is probably his decrease in monosyllabity in the later groups. Some minor discrepancies may be caused by the occasional cases in which weak, normally unstressed words are emphasized by syntactical situation and punctuation so that they do receive stress—as with the first word in

And, sub/tly of / herself / contem/plative.

But in spite of the discrepancies, Rossetti's use of more strong words than Milton and Keats appears to be the main reason for his larger number of stressed syllables.

What devices or traits of style enabled Rossetti to include more strong words than Milton or Keats within the confines of a sonnet? Looking for the answer, one encounters a factor that could only have hindered the inclusion of those words. That is Rossetti's late tendency to favor strikingly polysyllabic words—words such as "reduplicate," "inexplicably," "reverberant," "inveteracy," and "regenerate." Sometimes he managed to get two or three words of three or more syllables into a single line:

As instantaneous penetrating sense

Amulet, talisman, and oracle

Like multiform circumfluence manifold

Of some inexorable supremacy.

The reason why the later sonnets are less monosyllabic than the earlier sonnets is the use of these longer words, not the use of two-syllable words—for Rossetti never used as many of the latter as Milton or Keats. Where he is not monosyllabic, he tends not toward disyllabic moderation but toward a polysyllabic extreme.

This mannerism of diction is open to criticism—on the grounds that it is uneconomical, for one thing, since three or four shorter words might have said more than one polysyllable. But this complaint hardly stands up, because the sonnets include so high a proportion of strong words in spite of the polysyllables. Ornateness might be another ground for objecting to the polysyllables. Yet Rossetti did show restraint by using them only in some sonnets, not in all, and by seldom introducing more than three or four of the words into a single sonnet. And what seems ornate to some might be regarded by others as a touch of elevation and elegance appropriate to the formal style of the sonnets. Moreover, the polysyllables produce metrical variety because they generally result in a line with only three stressed syllables. And since all the stress of the line is concentrated on those syllables, they tend to be uttered with an intensity that lends unusual rhetorical force to the key words in which they occur:

> Hŏw pássionately and irretríevably.

Nevertheless—to return to the central question—such words do make it more difficult to produce a sonnet containing a high proportion of stressed syllables. Rossetti could have accomplished this only by increased condensation to eliminate weak words elsewhere in the poem.

He sometimes did this by simply omitting words that another poet might have included, as in the "Introductory Sonnet":

> A Sonnet is a moment's monument,—
> [A] Memorial from the Soul's eternity
> To one dead [but] deathless hour. Look that it be,
> Whether for [a] lustral rite or [for a] dire portent,
> Of its own arduous fulness reverent.

More often Rossetti condensed by using modifying words instead of phrases or clauses—"one dead deathless hour" instead of "one hour that is dead but deathless." The most frequent example of this trait is the use of inflected noun genitives rather than genitive phrases—"moment's monument" and "Soul's eternity" instead of "monument of a moment" and "eternity of the Soul." Besides these instances the "Introductory Sonnet" contains "Love's . . . retinue," "wharf's . . .

breath," and "Charon's palm," but only one phrase, "appeals of life." As another example, Sonnet LXXXVIII contains "Eros' name," "Leander's sake," "dawn's . . . light," "Death's neophyte," "Anteros' . . . shrine," and "life's love," and but one genitive phrase, "issue . . . of a . . . love." These two sonnets are not unusual in this regard, for the practice became habitual with Rossetti: in his Group IV sonnets 72 per cent of the noun genitives are inflected, compared with only 46 per cent of Milton's and 44 per cent of Keats's, both of whom favored genitive phrases.

Another important means of condensation was the use of compound words such as "chaff-strewn" instead of "strewn like chaff," "wood-notes" instead of "notes in a wood," "stream-fed" instead of "fed by a stream," "dream-dowered," "angel-trodden," and many others. These too became a distinctive trait of Rossetti's sonnets (as they later did in the poetry of Hopkins), especially since, as with the polysyllabic words, he liked to put two or three of them into a single line:

> Like frost-bound fire-girt scenes of long ago
>
> The storm-felled forest-trees moss-grown today
>
> One flame-winged met a white-winged harp-player.

When one observes the number of stressed syllables in the lines above (seven, seven, and eight respectively), the tendency of compound terms to produce a strongly stressed sonnet is obvious.

Rossetti's purpose in using these devices of syntactical condensation was probably not so much metrical as emotional. That is, he was not trying primarily to write strongly stressed verse—although he was surely aware of that result; rather, he was trying to introduce more words conveying strong feelings. Metrically weak words such as prepositions and conjunctions express relations between ideas, but metrically strong words express the ideas themselves—ideas of persons, objects, actions, and qualities. And these ideas arouse emotions. Consequently, increasing the number of stressed words goes hand in hand with increasing the sonnet's content of meaning and feeling. In this regard Rossetti's advantage over Milton and Keats—an average of from three to six strong words per sonnet—may not seem large enough to matter. But the sonnets of those poets are themselves plentiful in ideas and emotions, to say the least. And when one turns from the average to the particular, Rossetti's advantage is still more impressive: although some of his sonnets contain no more strong words than most of Milton's and Keats's, others contain ten to fifteen more—which makes them packed indeed.

Certainly the result is not necessarily a better poem; excellence depends on the quality of ideas, not on the quantity, and no Rossetti sonnet surpasses the best of Milton and Keats. In fact, too many ideas may clog the movement of a sonnet, too many emotions may cloy one's sensitivity like a mass of flowers in a greenhouse, and too much condensation to make room for ideas may cause obscurity—as it does in some of Rossetti's sonnets. But at least such concentration bears out one of the few claims Rossetti made about his writing: "As a result of my method of composition, my work becomes condensed. Probably the man does not live who could write what I have written more briefly than I have done."[6] And most of his sonnets offer a rich but not overabundant train of ideas that creates a moving experience.

Still another trait of Rossetti's style is pointed to when the strong words in the groups of sonnets are classified according to parts of speech. The following table shows the average number per sonnet of the four main classes, including related participial forms (interjections are not shown because they average fewer than one per sonnet):

	Nouns	Adjectives	Verbs	Adverbs
M.	29.2	14.7	14.3	6.6
K.	26.2	19.1	10.5	6.6
R.—I	26.8	13.8	13.7	9.4
II	29	17.2	10.9	8.1
III	31.8	20.4	8.8	6.7
IV	32.1	20.2	9.8	5.5

When only the noun column is considered, the differences among the poets correspond fairly well to the differences in their total number of strong words of all kinds. Keats has the smallest total and the fewest nouns; Milton has a larger total and more nouns; and as Rossetti's total increases chronologically, the number of his nouns also increases to an amount larger than Milton's. But the adjective and verb columns indicate a more significant trait. Keats, despite

6. Caine, *Recollections*, p. 221.

his smaller total of strong words, uses more adjectives than Milton; this is made possible because he uses fewer verbs. Rossetti's earliest sonnets are similar to Milton's in having fewer adjectives and more verbs than other groups; but his later groups move toward and beyond Keats's practice, with an increase in adjectives and a decrease in verbs, together with a consequent decrease in adverbs.

This indicates that Milton tended to write verbal sonnets concerned with actions—sonnets in which the Lord avenges and men "serve who only stand and wait." So did Rossetti, in his earliest period. But his later sonnets became adjectival like Keats's, more static and pictorial, with persons and objects that tend more to possess qualities than to perform actions—the scenic sonnets of a painter in which "hands lie open in the long, fresh grass" with finger-points "like rosy blooms," and the "moment's monument" that symbolizes a sonnet has a "flowering crest impearled and orient." These are relative differences, of course—a matter of more or less description or action, not of all or none; and they are average differences—some individual sonnets are exceptions to them. But they nevertheless constitute an important development in Rossetti's style.

To return to characteristics that are more strictly metrical: the analysis of the number of stressed syllables in the sonnets has led to significant traits of diction and method, but it is only the beginning of a description of the meter. We need to discover more about the kind and degree of metrical irregularity. That is, a sonnet with 74 stressed syllables, Rossetti's average in the later groups, might contain four spondees and no pyrrhics—an extremely regular meter; or it might contain fourteen spondees and ten pyrrhics (or thirteen and nine, and so on)—a very different, markedly irregular meter. The following table gives the average number of pyrrhics and spondees per sonnet and, to indicate the total amount of irregularity, their combined sum:

	Pyrrhics	Spondees	Total
M.	5.5	7.3	12.8
K.	9.6	7.9	17.5
R.—I	8.6	10.7	19.3
II	7.2	11.2	18.4
III	7.7	12.6	20.3
IV	7.9	12.2	20.1

Although Milton is far from being a cautiously regular metrist, he is the most regular of the three, using the fewest pyrrhics and spondees, with a slight advantage in spondees. Keats averages about five more irregular feet than Milton and, consistent with his lower proportion of stressed syllables, most of this advantage is in pyrrhics.[7] His verse tends to be the most light and swift. Rossetti is the least regular and tends in the opposite direction from Keats—increasingly so in the later groups; averaging fewer pyrrhics than Keats, though more than Milton, and from four to five more spondees than either, he writes the most heavily stressed, slowest verse.

But again some individual poems vary considerably from these averages. To what extent is shown in the table below, which gives the actual number of pyrrhics and spondees for the sonnet in each group that is most regular (having the fewest pyrrhics and spondees combined), for the one that is most irregular (having the most pyrrhics and spondees combined), for the one that is lightest in stress (having the largest advantage of pyrrhics over spondees), and for the one that is heaviest in stress (having the largest advantage of spondees over pyrrhics):

	Most Regular		Most Irregular		Lightest		Heaviest	
	P.	Sp.	P.	Sp.	P.	Sp.	P.	Sp.
M.	3	5	13	6	13	6	4	14
K.	5	5	10	14	14	6	5	11
R.—I	7	7	10	18	12	7	3	12
II	3	10	11	14	12	10	5	17
III	5	9	11	17	13	9	3	20
IV	5	9	8	18	15	6	8	18

As the table indicates, not every sonnet of Rossetti's is highly irregular and heavily stressed, not every one of Keats's is less irregular and lightly stressed, and not every one of Milton's is relatively regular. Rossetti does write the heaviest individual sonnet, with seventeen more spondees than pyrrhics, but he also writes the lightest, with nine more pyrrhics than spondees. He does write the most ir-

7. Walter Jackson Bate, in *The Stylistic Development of Keats* (New York, 1962), p. 120, finds 9.3 per cent spondees in the later sonnets of Keats, whereas my finding here amounts to 11 per cent. The difference may be due to a difference in the sonnets that constitute my group. In any case it is so slight, about one spondee per sonnet, that it indicates a close agreement in our scansion.

regular sonnets, with as many as twenty-eight pyrrhics and spondees, but he also writes sonnets that are considerably more regular
than some of Milton's and Keats's. Nevertheless the variations in
these exceptional sonnets—an extreme variation in the case of Rossetti—do not contradict the tendencies indicated by the average
figures of the preceding table. A Rossetti sonnet will generally be
more irregular, most often in the direction of heaviness, than one by
Milton or Keats.

While average figures tend to conceal the traits of individual sonnets, even the actual figures for individual sonnets may tend to mis-
lead by suggesting that irregularities such as spondees and pyrrhics
are distributed evenly throughout a poem. Usually they are not.
Most of the sonnets of all three poets contain enough irregular feet
so that every line might have one or more; however, in nearly every
sonnet there are lines, often several lines, that contain none and
other lines that contain three or four. This trait is especially notice-
able in Rossetti. Whether by instinct or design, whether as a conse-
quence of word choice or of an effort to shape meter, he tends to
cluster spondees and sometimes pyrrhics into concentrations. As a
result one finds, not a moderately irregular, moderately heavy
meter throughout, but unusually heavy lines and passages among
other lines that are regular or that are exceptionally light.

To describe that trait of clustering, along with other qualities of
the meter, I will use a concept that I call a "stress-height." By that
term I mean any stressed syllable or any series of consecutive
stressed syllables. A regular iambic line can be said to have five
stress-heights:

He stooped / o'er sweet / Colon/na's dy/ing head.

A line regular except for an initial inverted foot also has five:

City, / of thine / a sin/gle sim/ple door.

And a line regular except for an initial spondee has five, but the
first is a two-syllable stress-height:

How strange / a thing / to be / what man / can know.

One inverted foot within a line reduces the number of stress-heights to four, one of which is two syllables long:

To <u>feel</u> / the <u>first</u> / <u>kiss</u> and / for<u>bode</u> / the <u>last</u>.

And a pyrrhic reduces the number to four without lengthening any:

I <u>crave</u> / the <u>ref</u>/uge of / her <u>deep</u> / em<u>brace</u>.

There is no reason to regard the examples above as anything but iambic meter, regular in the first line, slightly irregular in the others. But the case is different with such a line as

The <u>wave-/bowered pearl</u>, / the <u>heart-/shaped seal</u> / of <u>green</u>.

Here spondees in the second and fourth positions produce a line having three stress-heights, with each of the first two stress-heights being three syllables in length and the third being one syllable in length. The dominant rhythm of the line is a rhythm of three oscillations—three rises and falls between each of the three unstressed syllables and the stress-height that follows each of those syllables. It is best to describe the line as having a "stress-height rhythm" rather than to describe it as irregular iambic. The reason is that although the iambic meter does continue to exist in the line, it is different from the stress-height rhythm and less prominent. It continues to exist because the second syllable in every metrical foot, including the spondees that constitute part of the first two stress-heights, is stronger than the first syllable:

The <u>wáve-/bôwered péarl</u>, / the <u>héart-/shâped séal</u> / of <u>gréen</u>.

Thus the line has an iambic pattern of five oscillations between weaker syllables and stronger syllables, along with the more prominent stress-height rhythm of three oscillations between unstressed syllables and stress-heights. But if Rossetti had written

The <u>péarl</u> / <u>wáve-bôwered</u>, / the <u>séal</u> / of <u>gréen</u> / <u>héart-shâped</u>,

the line would still have a stress-height rhythm of three oscillations, but it would lose its iambic quality because the second syllable in each of the two spondees is now weaker than the first syllable rather than stronger. In a much lighter line one also finds a stress-height rhythm of three oscillations, but because all the stress-heights are only one syllable in length they are less prominent and the rhythm is less strongly felt:

From leth/argy / to fev/er of / the heart.

Again the iambic pattern of a weaker syllable followed by a stronger syllable is maintained in all feet, including the pyrrhics in the intervals between stress-heights.

It is true that within the spondees and pyrrhics of the preceding examples the second syllable is only slightly stronger than the first —the difference between them is much smaller than in a regular iamb. But that does not nullify the iambic meter; it only explains why it becomes subordinate to the stress-height rhythm, like wavelets that are taken up as part of a larger swell. It is also true that one can find cases in which an iambic reading is not inevitable—in some spondees and pyrrhics the first syllable might be stressed as strongly as the second or more strongly. But with few exceptions an iambic reading, with the second syllable stronger than the first, can be given without unnaturalness; and to give it is simply to make a normal concession to the metrical basis of the poem.

Just when a line can be said to have a stress-height rhythm different from and dominant over its iambic meter cannot be defined exactly; it depends upon a reader's sensitivity to rhythm. But most readers should feel it in any line having three stress-heights or fewer, especially when one or more stress-heights is two or more syllables long. Rossetti wrote literally hundreds of such lines. Below are a few examples, with the iambic shown by scansion marks and the stress-heights underlined:

Or mock/ing winds / whirl round / a chaff-/strewn floor

Neath bower-/linked arch / of white / arms glor/ified

The loves / that from / his hand / proud youth / lets fall

And girls / whom none / call maid/ens laugh,— / strange road[8]

8. A stress-height that includes a punctuated pause obviously differs some-

The spir/its of / thy mourn/ful min/isterings
Carve it / in i/vory / or in eb/ony.

But of course Rossetti was not the only poet to use stress-height rhythm. Lines that exhibit it are fairly common in poetry—for example, Sidney's

With how / sad steps, / O Moon, / thou climb'st / the skies,

and the line in which the monosyllabity of lines like Sidney's is derided by Pope—

And ten / low words / oft creep / in one / dull line

(an interesting line metrically, despite Pope's purpose of exemplifying dullness). Both Milton and Keats wrote many such lines.[9] What is important, then, is not that Rossetti used stress-height rhythm but that he used it more frequently and more prominently than those poets—and, it seems safe to say, than most other poets also.

Since stress-heights become more prominent as they become fewer, the smaller the number of stress-heights in a sonnet, the larger the number of lines in which stress-height rhythm will be felt. In comparison with the 70 stress-heights of a perfectly regular sonnet, Milton averages 60. Keats averages about five fewer (55.2). Rossetti averages about the same number as Keats in his two earliest groups (55.6), slightly fewer in the later groups (III–53.9, IV–54.8). But length also makes stress-heights more prominent. And since Rossetti introduces an average of about six more stressed syllables per sonnet into about the same number of stress-heights as Keats, considerably more of his stress-heights tend to be prominently long. Where Milton uses an average of about 53 stress-heights of one syllable (as in regular meter) and Keats somewhat

what from one that does not—perhaps enough in the case of a full stop to regard it as two stress-heights. But to consider that factor would complicate my present comparison unduly and, I think, unprofitably.

9. Keats wrote one remarkable line having ten stressed syllables, constituting a single stress-height: "Lo! who dares say, 'Do this'? Who dares call down" ("To a Young Lady Who Sent Me a Laurel Crown"). But lacking unstressed intervals, the line hardly exhibits stress-height rhythm; it is iambic, with its oscillations restricted to the two stronger levels of stress.

fewer (49), Rossetti uses still fewer (41). Of more prominent, two-syllable stress-heights, Milton averages fewest (4.4), and both Keats (4.8) and Rossetti (5.5) average slightly more. But with conspicuously long stress-heights of three or more syllables—a single one of which is often sufficient to endow a line with stress-height rhythm —Rossetti has a decided advantage. While Milton averages 2.8 per sonnet and Keats 2.9, he averages 6.3. As a result of his stress-heights being both long and few in number, about three more lines would exhibit stress-height rhythm in an average sonnet of Rossetti's than in an average sonnet of Keats's, and about five more than in an average sonnet of Milton's.

Perhaps the metrical traits that have been presented statistically may be made more concrete by describing a hypothetical average sonnet of Rossetti's. It would contain about three regular or nearly regular lines (M. 5, K. 4) having no more than one irregular foot— perhaps an initial inverted foot or spondee. Five or six lines would be moderately irregular (M. 7 or 8, K. 6 or 7), with one or two irregular feet; in some of these lines an internal spondee producing a three-syllable stress-height might create a feeling of stress-height rhythm. Four to six lines would be markedly irregular (M. 1 or 2, K. 3 or 4), with enough irregular feet to result in three or (in Rossetti more often than in Keats, and rarely in Milton) only two stress-heights. In virtually all of these lines stress-height rhythm would be prominent.

An average sonnet, however, is only an illustrative abstraction from which, to repeat a caveat, every individual sonnet varies. One might find some Rossetti sonnets that differ little in metrical style from most of those of the other poets; one can find others in which the Rossettian traits are much more pervasive than in the average sonnet just described. To provide a more specific idea of Rossetti's meter, examples are necessary. And they are necessary also to illustrate something more important than meter per se: the aesthetic effects that meter helps to produce in the poetry.

One of those aesthetic effects is a constant feeling of variety. Rossetti never lets one's rhythmic sensitivity fall into the kind of coma that can be produced by soporifically regular meter. In almost any of his sonnets one can find an example of a highly varied movement like that in the following passage, in which stress-heights are underlined:

And as / the trav/eller tri/umphs with / the sun,
Glorying / in heat's / mid-height, / yet star/tide brings
Wonder / new-born, / and still / fresh trans/port springs
From lim/pid lam/bent hours / of day / begun.

The first line, with three brief stress-heights, is very light (and consequently the "traveller" moves swiftly); the next two, with their longer stress-heights, are much heavier and slower; and the last line, being contrastingly regular, also contributes to the variety.

Stress-height rhythm arises from metrical irregularity—a term that may connote roughness. But the rhythm is anything but rough. Since its risings and fallings are fewer, longer, and slower than the trotting oscillations of regular iambic, they tend to produce smooth, flowing lines. And with suitable subject matter such lines create an impression of undulant gracefulness, as in these passages describing a lovely lady and her pastoral surroundings in the well-known sonnet "Silent Noon":

Your hands / lie o/pen in / the long / fresh grass,—
The fin/ger-points / look through / like ros/y blooms:
Your eyes / smile peace. / The pas/ture gleams / and glooms

.   .   .   .

Deep in / the sun-/searched growths / the drag/on-fly
Hangs like / a blue / thread loos/ened from / the sky.

To realize how greatly the beauty of this poem depends on its meter, one need only translate some lines into more regular meter and feel that beauty disappear:

Your hands / are ly/ing o/pen in / the grass,
The fin/ger-points / appear / like ros/y blooms:
Your eyes / are smil/ing peace. / The pas/ture gleams. . . .

And so on, into monotony. Perhaps some of what is lost in the second version is semantic—a result of deleting "long" and "fresh" in the first line. But those words do not express ideas that are especially striking; one feels that Rossetti introduced them mainly to add grace and strength to the meter.

As was indicated in the hypothetical average sonnet, stress-height rhythm is not continuous throughout entire sonnets of Rossetti's. It emerges from the more regular iambic and subsides again, becoming apparent in about one-third to one-half of the lines (but in as many as two-thirds in some sonnets). Nor is there a systematic pattern in which those lines are distributed, or any special kind of subject matter for which they are used. They do, however, tend to be most frequent in passages where emotion is strongest. The reason is simply that Rossetti tends to produce the emotion by an unusual concentration of words which, being emotionally strong, are also metrically strong. This means more spondees, fewer and longer stress-heights, and stress-height rhythm. Also, it is in such passages that he is most prone to employ a few polysyllabic words, which again produce fewer, though shorter, stress-heights and stress-height rhythm. These polysyllables, as was said earlier, achieve a peculiar rhetorical force because so much of the line's stress is concentrated on their one emphatically uttered syllable. On the other hand, in lines in which numerous stressed monosyllables are combined into long stress-heights, the prolonged forceful utterance—like a raised tone of voice—also creates more emphasis and feeling than utterance oscillating in an even five beats per line. Thus both kinds of stress-height rhythm tend to augment emotion, as in this passage describing a person's momentous return to a scene of his early life:

> What place / so strange,— / though un/reveal/èd snow
> With un/imag/ina/ble fires / arise
> At the / earth's end,— / what pas/sion of / surprise
> Like frost-/bound fire-/girt scenes / of long / ago?

In another example, a description of the fatal enticements of the seductress Lilith, a brief passage of heavy stress-height lines between more regular lines considerably enhances the mood of dramatic ominousness:

> The rose / and pop/py are / her flowers; / for where
> Is he / not found, / O Lil/ith, whom / shed scent
> And soft-/shed kis/ses and / soft sleep / shall snare?
> Lo! as / that youth's / eyes burned / at thine, / so went
> Thy spell / through him, / and left / his straight / neck bent
> And round / his heart / one stran/gling gold/en hair.

The intensification produced by extended stress-heights can be seen when the last line above, one of the less forceful, is made much less forceful by changing its longest stress-height into two short stress-heights,

And <u>round</u> / his <u>heart</u> / a <u>stran</u>/gling <u>gold</u>/en <u>hair</u>.

Undoubtedly Rossetti recognized this dramatic value of sustained heavy stress and sought it: he certainly did not use "shed" in both the second and third lines above for the little that it says as much as for its contribution to stress (together with its contribution to the sibilant alliteration that characterizes the insidious Lilith).

In a final example, a heavy stress-height rhythm is maintained through the entire sestet of a sonnet. One can feel its cumulative force helping to dramatize Rossetti's feelings about the awesome knowledge revealed to Shelley after his death:

When <u>that</u> / mist <u>cleared</u>, / O <u>Shel</u>/ley! what /<u>dread veil</u>
Was <u>rent</u> / for <u>thee</u>, / to <u>whom</u> / far-dark/ling <u>Truth</u>
<u>Reigned sov</u>/ereign <u>guide</u> / through <u>thy</u> / brief age-/less <u>youth</u>?
Was the / <u>Truth thy</u> / <u>Truth</u>, Shel/ley?—<u>Hush</u>! / <u>All-Hail</u>!
Past <u>doubt</u>, / thou <u>gav'st</u> / it; and / in <u>Truth's</u> / <u>bright sphere</u>
Art <u>first</u> / of <u>prais</u>/ers, being / <u>most prais</u>/èd <u>here</u>.

In a large part of Rossetti's sonnet verse, as in the passages above, the rhythm seems to rise and fall as naturally and freely as if controlled only by the emotion of the subject matter; indeed, it sometimes seems dangerously close to breaking loose from metrical rule. But it never does break quite loose—and that reservation is crucial. As I made a point of showing earlier, Rossetti maintains the iambic meter even within extended stress-heights and extended weak intervals between stress-heights. Consequently one always feels the actual rhythm as a divergence in greater or lesser degree from that iambic base. Now, free verse, accentual meters like Hopkins' sprung rhythm, and even a good deal of prose might be said to have stress-height rhythm, but these do not produce such a feeling of divergence because, of course, they have no base meter from which to diverge. So they gain their rhythmic freedom at the cost of an important quality that is captured when a base meter is maintained. That is the tension created as the actual rhythm of the language continually strains away from and returns toward its abstract metrical base—a tension that constitutes part of the total emotion. Rossetti retained that quality and added to it—by achieving a movement which, in its remarkable variety, often seems as unconfined as spontaneous speech, and by making the variations of that movement reinforce the subject matter, not only as an occasional "echo to the sense" but as a pervasive and powerful element in creating the mood and drama of the poetry.

Apart from sonnets and ballads, most of Rossetti's poems are written in an iambic tetrameter that exhibits many of the traits of the sonnets' pentameter, but to a lesser degree. For example, one comes upon lines that are extraordinarily heavy in stress,

> So pure,—so fall'n! How dare to think
>
> Nay, Nay, mere words. Here nothing warns,

and occasional lines that are startlingly light,

> Aparelled beyond parallel
> An eligible deity.

Containing more spondees than pyrrhics, the verse tends like that of the sonnets to be heavier than the verse of other poets: of three poems in tetrameter couplets, Rossetti's "Jenny" contains 13.8 per cent spondees and 10.6 per cent pyrrhics, Browning's "The Italian in England" has 11.6 per cent spondees and 11 per cent pyrrhics, and Keats's "The Eve of St. Mark" has 8.2 per cent spondees and 13.1 per cent pyrrhics. But the percentage of spondees in "Jenny" and other Rossetti poems in tetrameter is smaller than in the sonnets (16.7 per cent), and so is the percentage of other kinds of irregular feet. The reason is simply that fewer of those feet are needed in the shorter line to create an equivalent impression of irregularity. Also, the shorter line does not allow enough room for the longer oscillations needed to produce the sonnets' effect of stressheight rhythm. On the whole, then, the tetrameter verse is skillful, varied, and pleasing, but its Rossettian traits are not as frequently and prominently apparent. The most distinctive meter outside the sonnets is the meter of the ballads.

BALLAD METER

Although Rossetti is better known for his sonnets, his ballad pro-
duction is impressive—eight principal poems totaling nearly three
thousand lines; and the best of them, "Sister Helen," "The Staff and
Scrip," and "Rose Mary," are excelled by only a handful of English
ballads such as "The Rime of the Ancient Mariner," "La Belle Dame
Sans Merci," and "The Lady of Shalott." What is more, he was an
important innovator in ballad technique. Hall Caine credited him
with an influence that, as it happened, turned out somewhat to Rossetti's disadvantage: "Certain of Rossetti's ballads, whilst still un-
known to the public, so far influenced contemporary poetry that
when they did at length appear they had all the appearance to the
uninitiated of work imitated from contemporary models, instead of
being, as in fact they were, the primary source of inspiration for
writers whose names were established earlier."[10] One of the influences Caine had in mind must have been Rossetti's revival and further development of the refrain stanza and of the question-and-response narrative method, both derived from the folk poem "Edward,
Edward"—devices that Swinburne and Morris employed later and
that continued to be used by Yeats, Kipling, and others. Another in-
novation of Rossetti's was metrical. "There lies your line," he is re-
ported to have told himself when he first became acquainted with
the old ballads,[11] and in a sense he did make the line his own by
achieving the closest reproduction of folk meter to be found in literary ballads.

What are the folk traits that needed to be reproduced? One of
them is the stanza. "Edward, Edward" and a few other folk poems
employ a stanza having two four-beat lines with intervening refrain
lines. Five of Rossetti's ballads use only four-beat lines, and three of
these have those lines arranged into refrain stanzas. A much more
common folk form is the four-line stanza having alternating four-
beat and three-beat lines, with the second and fourth lines rhyming
($a^4b^3c^4b^3$). Many literary ballads employ that form, including some
of Rossetti's. Another trait often cited as a ballad characteristic is a
pronounced medial caesura in the four-beat lines, often with an internal rhyme at that point, as in "The guests are met, the feast is

10. *Recollections,* p. 41.
11. T. Hall Caine, *Recollections of Rossetti* (London, 1928), p. 247 (a revised edition of *Recollections of Dante Gabriel Rossetti,* referred to above).

set." But the frequent use of such lines is more a trait of Coleridge in "The Rime of the Ancient Mariner" than of folk ballads. They do occur in the old poems, but only infrequently, and the same is true in most of Rossetti's ballads. One distinctive Rossettian borrowing from folk ballads, which was also adopted by Morris, is the device of ending an occasional line with a two-syllable word, accented normally on the first syllable, which requires some shifting of accent to get the required metrical stress on the final syllable (a process that will be discussed more fully in the chapter on rhyme). In folk ballads these terms are most often stock terms or names:

> Was not in all the north *countrée*
>
> And they away to the greene *forrèst*
>
> And ever I pray you, Child *Waters*.[12]

Lines ending with such terms average about one in twenty in folk ballads, though of course the frequency varies in different poems. No literary ballad has that many, and most have none. "The Rime of the Ancient Mariner" contains three in 625 lines, the stock term *countree* each time. Rossetti used them in most ballads, and at a higher frequency than Coleridge: "Rose Mary" contains eight in 830 lines, plus ten terminal words like *moorside* and *footfall* in which the weaker second syllable requires enough shifting of normal accent so that they resemble the ballad terms. But Rossetti deviated from folk practice by using original terms rather than stock terms:

> Till day lies dead on the sun-*dial*
>
> In a coiling serpent's life-*likeness*
>
> And the water's bright through the dart-*rushes*.

Moreover, he sometimes used them in sonnets and other poems besides ballads—a practice that made them something of a trademark of his. In his ballads these endings introduce a touch of quaint authenticity; however, they are not frequent enough in either folk

12. Thomas Percy, *Reliques of Ancient English Poetry* (London, 1857), has been used in this study as the source of all quotations and the basis of all analysis of folk ballads. Rossetti was familiar with this work (*Family-Letters*, I, 98).

ballads or Rossetti's ballads to constitute an important general trait of meter.

What is much more important, because it is constant rather than occasional, is the basic quality of folk meter. Since it is always a rising meter, with most often only one unstressed syllable preceding each stressed syllable, it can be regarded as iambic. But it is usually a most irregular iambic, because it contains numerous anapests and sometimes even feet with three unstressed syllables before the strong syllable:

> Leave off / the brýt/lyng of the déar, / he sáyde,
>
> And to your bówys / look ye táyk / good héed;
>
> For név/er sithe ye wéar / on your móth/ars bórne
>
> Had ye név/er so míck/le néed.

A singer could manage the four-syllable feet smoothly by shortening their sounds and prolonging other feet to compensate, but they make a modern reader stumble. A second stumbling block is an occasional line having consecutive strong syllables that cause a reader, lacking a singer's familiarity with the poem, to be uncertain about which syllable receives the principal stress. He may come out with five principal beats,

> I név/er húrt / fair máid / in áll / my tíme,

instead of the four beats that the metrical pattern demands,

> I név/er hurt faír / maid in áll / my time.

A literary imitation of the folk meter, then, should have numerous anapests but, to avoid confusing a reader, no feet having more than three syllables and no lines in which the position of the principal stresses is uncertain. Finally—a most important quality—the anapests must give the impression of occurring at random in any part of the line; it is this trait that gives the folk meter its spontaneity and freedom.

The number of anapests varies in different folk ballads, tending to be greater in the older poems. A typical example, "The Ancient Ballad of Chevy Chase," averages about seventy-five anapests per hundred lines, or three in every four-line stanza. In contrast, "The More Modern Ballad of Chevy Chase," an anonymous sixteenth-century literary version of the same tale, is in "correct" iambic; it employs no anapests and utterly loses the spontaneity of folk meter. On the other hand, that spontaneity is also lost in such a ballad as Sir Walter Scott's "Lochinvar," which has a basic anapestic meter that moves at too methodical a gallop. Coleridge, in "The Rime of the Ancient Mariner," comes closer to the folk meter, although his average of seventeen anapests per hundred lines is conservative. The frequency of anapests in Rossetti's ballads is as follows:

	Anapests (or dactyls in trochaic lines) per hundred lines
Jan Van Hunks (1846)	65
Dennis Shand (1850)	28
Sister Helen (1851)	73
The Staff and Scrip (1852)	7
Stratton Water (1854)	17
Troy Town (1869)	57
Eden Bower (1869)	114
Rose Mary (1871)	61
The White Ship (1880)	111
The King's Tragedy (1881)	83

As a young poet Rossetti was sometimes conservative with anapests, sometimes boldly experimental. In two early poems, "Dennis Shand" (which he decided against publishing) and "Stratton Water," his moderate amount of anapests is closer to the practice of Coleridge than to folk meter. (The striking scarcity of anapests in "The Staff and Scrip" is a special case that will be discussed presently.) But still earlier, and apparently with no precedent in literary ballads, he had imitated the folk ballads' liberal scattering of anapests in writing the first part of "Jan Van Hunks"—a proportion that he maintained when he completed the poem just before his death.[13] Obviously he liked that effect, for he used the same meter, only slightly more anapestic, in his first published ballad, "Sister Helen." And virtually the same meter, with another moderate increase in anapests, occurs in the late ballad "The King's Tragedy":

13. *Dante Gabriel Rossetti: Jan Van Hunks*, ed. John Robert Wahl (New York, 1952).

O Gód! / what móre / did I héar / or sée,
Or hów / should I téll / the rést?
But thére / at léngth / our kíng / lay sláin
With síx/teen woúnds / in his bréast.

There were good reasons for adopting the meter. The swift movement produced by the anapests, caused by their effect of rushing over two unstressed syllables in the time normally given to one syllable, suits the tales of action for which Rossetti used it. The unpatterned distribution of the anapests can create an effect of artless naturalness and sincerity. Variety was another reason: usually every line in refrain stanzas and every second and fourth line in quatrains ends with a strong pause. The result is a steady rhythmic advance of short lines, couplets, and stanzas that in a long ballad—and some of Rossetti's are very long—tends to produce a monotony which the enlivening effect of anapests helps to counteract. It was certainly because of such advantages that Rossetti imitated folk meter, and not merely because of an antiquarian desire to re-establish a tradition. For if traditionalism had been his goal, he could be expected to have adhered to a close imitation of folk meter, once he had arrived at it, in all his ballads. Instead he deviated from it, while retaining some of its qualities, to suit the needs of several poems.

One example is "The White Ship," in which Rossetti used about thirty more anapests per hundred lines (111) than are normal in folk ballads or than he used in "The King's Tragedy"—also a long ballad of historical adventure and written at about the same time. The reason appears to have been the poem's stanzas. Whereas those of "The King's Tragedy" are varied—quatrains, quintains, and sestets, containing both tetrameter and trimeter lines—those of "The White Ship" are of only two or occasionally three lines, all tetrameter. These court the monotony—in fact, they probably capture it—to which a long poem in short stanzas is prone. It was probably in an effort to mitigate this tendency that Rossetti used so large a frequency of anapests.

In contrast, the early ballad "The Staff and Scrip" almost eschews anapests. The reason appears to have been the poem's subject matter and mood. It is a somber story of a knight who aids a queen by leading her forces to a victory in which he is killed, told mostly from the viewpoint of the queen as she accepts the knight's help, waits while the battle is fought, and grieves at his death—a tale not so much of action as of psychological tension and pain. Such a mood, Rossetti must have felt, called for a less lively movement than the usual ballad rhythm, for he avoided quatrains in favor of a slightly longer original stanza ($a^4b^3a^4b^3b^2$), and he limited anapests to only fifteen in more than two hundred lines. Significantly, he employed eight of these in one short passage (st. xxv–xxx) where they enliven a description of the principal action, the off-stage battle.

Again in "Rose Mary" Rossetti seems to have felt that the subject matter—a brooding tale of illicit love, betrayal, deception by evil spirits, retribution, and death—called for some restraint of the rhythm. Consequently he devised a stanza ($aabbb^4$) that is half again as long as a ballad quatrain and much less lively. And though he did not curtail anapests as in "The Staff and Scrip," he used fewer (sixty-one per hundred lines) than in most of his later ballads. But he partly compensated for that limitation by an interesting device—the use of ionic feet (i.e., a pyrrhic followed by a spondee) as at the beginning of

Till the / fláme paĺed / to the red / sunrise.

Such a foot resembles an anapest in having two unstressed syllables preceding a stressed syllable ("Till the fláme"), and this produces an anapest's skipping effect. But the two consecutive stressed syllables prevent the impression of speed that an anapest produces. In iambic tetrameter poetry in general, such feet occur at an average of roughly one in fifteen lines. At the beginning of a line, a position where they become most prominent, they occur in only about one line in thirty.[14] And they are much rarer in ballad verse; only about one line in seventy-five begins with an ionic in folk ballads, fewer than one line in a hundred in "The Rime of the Ancient Mariner," and no more than that in most of Rossetti's ballads. Consequently their frequency in "Rose Mary"—in which they begin one line in twenty—is significantly high. Apparently Rossetti introduced them deliberately to add an occasional anapestic lilt without any undesirable increase in speed—for, as we will see, he used the same device for the same purpose in "The Blessed Damozel."

Another unusual metrical trait appears in "Rose Mary"—numer-

14. A generous estimate based on 260 lines of Keats's "The Eve of Saint Mark" and Browning's "The Italian in England." In the first 500 lines of Tennyson's *In Memoriam* initial ionics average 1 in 63 lines.

ous lines that are trochaic through the first half or three-fourths of
their length but that return to iambic before the end. Rare examples
can be found in folk ballads:

> Bomen / bickarte / uppone / the bent
> Hardyar / men both / off hart / nor hand.

And Rossetti had used two such lines in "Sister Helen":

> Flank to / flank are / the three / steeds gone
> See her / now or / never / see aught.

In "Rose Mary" they are remarkably frequent, averaging one line
in ten, and sometimes two occur in a single stanza:

> Mother, / something / flashed to / my sight!—
> Nay, it / is but / the lap/wing's flight.—
> What glints / there like / a lance / that flees?—
> Nay, the / flags are / stirred in / the breeze,
> And the wat/er's bright / through the dart-/rushes.

At the point where these lines return from trochaic to iambic the
two unstressed syllables before a stressed syllable ("to my sight")
produce an anapestic effect appropriate to the poem. What is more,
the frequent brief changes in meter create a shifting, elusive quality
that accords well with "Rose Mary's" theme of intrigue and deception.

Like "Sister Helen," in which a woman ruthlessly pursues a mur-
derous vengeance against a lover who jilted her, the two refrain
ballads that Rossetti wrote nearly twenty years later concern fe-
males driven by evil desire. Poems of pounding passion, they might
be called, with Helen, in "Troy Town," obsessively beseeching
Venus to grant satisfaction of her fiery lust for Paris, and Lilith, in
"Eden Bower," just as obsessively entreating the serpent to help
her, in exchange for her sexual favors, in getting revenge against
Adam and Eve. In both poems much of the pounding and the passion comes from the meter.

Unlike the meter of folk ballads and of Rossetti's other ballads,
that of "Troy Town" and "Eden Bower" is predominantly trochaic,

presumably chosen for its tendency to produce a more prominent beat than iambic. In "Troy Town" Rossetti emphasized that tendency by truncating the lines so that they end as well as begin with a stressed syllable. The meter's accompanying tendency toward a kind of metronomic monotony he forestalled by two main devices that create variety. He introduced a ballad-style scattering of trisyllabic feet (dactyls, at the rate of fifty-seven per one hundred lines). And he made the refrain lines contrastingly short, with long, evenly stressed vowels. The beating, skipping meter of the narrative lines lends a feeling of impetuous insistence to Helen's passionate pleas, and the recurring refrain lines, as they warn of the disastrous outcome of that passion, interrupt that urgent advance with their slower sounds:

> Sée my / breást, how / líke it / ís;
>
> (Ó Tróy Tówn!)
>
> Sée it / bare for the / air to / kiss!
>
> Ís the / cúp to thy / heárt's de/síre?
>
> Ó for the / breást, O / make it / hís!
>
> (Ó Tróy's dówn,
>
> Táll Tróy's on fíre!)

In "Eden Bower" the trochaic beat remains strong, even though Rossetti diminished it at the end of the lines by using feminine rhymes throughout. The meter is even more varied than in "Troy Town"—extraordinarily varied, in fact, with a very high frequency of 114 trisyllabic feet per 100 lines, with contrastingly short refrain lines again, and with iambic lines intermixed among the trochaic lines at a rate of one line in three. This mixing of meters results in one problem: the first syllable of every line must be unmistakably strong or unmistakably weak. If it is only moderately strong the reader does not know whether to stress it or not, since he does not know at the beginning of the line whether the line is meant to be trochaic or iambic. For example, in order to give the four beats per line that constitute the poem's rhythmic base, the first two lines of the poem must be read as

> Ít was / Lílith the / wífe of / Ádam:
>
> Nót a / dróp of her / blóod was / húman.

But a reader might fail to stress the initial syllables and come out with only three beats,

It was Líl/ith the wífe / of Ádam:

Not a dróp / of her blóod / was húman.

This matter bothered Rossetti, and he asked an opinion of Swinburne: "It rather troubles me that the first verse is readable in an inflexion not intended and may set the reader on a false tack of sound—i.e., he does not at once emphasize the first *it*. . . . Give me your opinion and don't damn me."[15] Swinburne advised him to let the verse stand.[16] Yet the problem may bother a reader, here and in perhaps three or four other lines of the poem.

But those are infrequent minor flaws, difficult to avoid, in an otherwise brilliantly effective meter. With its alternation between tetrameter narrative lines and trimeter refrain lines, with its shifting between rising and falling meter and between duple and triple feet, it has a remarkably free, restless movement that syncopates against the drumming of each line's fundamental beats. Its effect is to endow Lilith's chant of lasciviousness and hate with a feeling of primitive wildness, recurrently checked as in "Troy Town" by the refrains:

Lend thy / shápe for the / lóve of / Lílith!

(Alás the hoúr!)

Look, my / moúth and my / chéek are / rúddy,

And thóu / art cóld / and fíre / is my bódy.

Lend thy / shápe for the / háte of / Ádam!

(Síng Éden Bówer!)

That hé / may waíl / my jóy / that forsóok him,

And cúrse / the dáy / when the bríde-/sleep tóok him.

For the most part Rossetti's work exhibits a firm sense of genre, so that the meter of his ballads and the meter of his other poetry are distinctly different. But it would be surprising if his ballad writing had not affected his other poetry in some way. And one does find certain traits of his ballad meter in a few poems that are not

15. *Letters of Dante Gabriel Rossetti*, eds. Oswald Doughty and John Robert Wahl (Oxford, 1965), II, 807.   16. Ibid., II, 809n1.

ballads. One of those poems, "The Blessed Damozel," will be discussed later. The others are three lyrics written in the latter part of his career, "The Cloud Confines" (1871), "Parted Presence" (1875), and "Three Shadows" (1876). In all three the stanzas are fairly long, six lines or more, and the lines are shortened to trimeters. The meter is varied less by spondees and pyrrhics, as in most of the lyrics, and more by initial inverted feet and, especially, by the ballad device of frequent anapests, one for every line or two, distributed apparently at random. The resulting meter is less graceful than that of Rossetti's other lyric poems; rather it has the swift irregular quality of spontaneous language. And the terse, crisp lines, nearly all with three firm beats unweakened by pyrrhics, and nearly all ending with punctuation or with pauses strong enough to make each line a rhythmic unit, build up an aggressive, driving movement during the progress of the stanza:

> What of / the heart / of hate
> That beats / in thy breast, / O Time?—
> Red strife / from the furth/est prime,
> And an/guish of fierce / debate;
> War that / shatters / her slain,
> And peace / that grinds / them as grain,
> And eyes / fixed ev/er in vain
> On the pit/iless eyes / of fate.
> Still we / say as / we go,—
> "Strange to / think by / the way,
> Whatev/er there is / to know,
> That shall / we know / some day."
> ("The Cloud Confines")

Poets before Rossetti had written lyrics in a meter in which anapests are intermixed with iambs, of course—Blake, for example, in some of the "Songs," and Shelley in "The Cloud" and other poems. But none of those meters are quite like Rossetti's above; their anapests tend to be more frequent and to occur in a regular pattern—not at random, with the effect of accidents of speech. However, when one turns to later poetry one finds a meter very similar to Rossetti's in certain poems of Yeats:

> Maybe / a twelve/month since
> Sudden/ly I / began,

In scorn / of this aud/ience,
Imag/ining / a man,
And his / sun-freck/led face,
And grey / Connemar/a cloth,
Climbing / up to / a place
Where stone / is dark / under froth,
And the down-/turn of / his wrist
When the flies / drop in / the stream;
A man / who does not / exist,
A man / who is / but a dream;
And cried, / "Before / I am old
I shall / have writ/ten him one
Poem / maybe / as cold
And pas/sionate as / the dawn."
                    ("The Fisherman")

Yeats's stanza is even longer than Rossetti's, but its other main traits
are much the same—the same short, terse, mostly end-paused lines,
the same initial inversions, the same scattering of anapests. One
even finds in both examples the device that Rossetti first used frequently in "Rose Mary"—lines that begin with a shift from the predominant iambic to trochaic but that return to iambic before the
end. Rossetti has

War that / shatters / her slain
Still we / say as / we go
Strange to / think by / the way.

And Yeats has

Climbing / up to / a place
Poem / maybe / as cold.

Moreover other poets after Yeats have employed this "loose iambic" meter, as it has been called, in short lines arranged in long
stanzas—Auden, for example, uses in "September 1, 1939" a verse
with precisely the traits pointed to above. The various metrical
practices of Rossetti that have been shown in this chapter exhibit,
along with skill, a good deal of innovativeness. And it appears that
he also deserves credit for anticipating, perhaps even for influ-
encing, an important meter of half a century later.

2

Stanzaic Forms—Structure and Rhythm

MORE THAN most poets, Rossetti had a preference for stanzaic forms defined by rhymes—sonnets, continuous couplets, and various kinds of stanzas—as opposed to that perennially popular form, blank verse. The only important exception is his blank verse dramatic monologue, "A Last Confession." If one studies that poem for some clue—some lack of skill, perhaps—that explains why he did not use blank verse more often, one finds none. He had practiced that form as a child, and as a youth he had used it expertly in some brief travel descriptions. And the verse of "A Last Confession," although not outstanding, is thoroughly competent; no first-rate practitioner of the form would have seen cause to disown it.

So Rossetti's preference for stanzaic forms could only have been due to advantages he found in them. One of these was the rhyme sounds, which he found it possible to exploit by making them produce certain emotional effects that will be shown later in this study. And he also exploited the two main attributes that stanzaic forms possess to a greater extent than blank verse. One of these is structural or architectonic; the other is rhythmic. That is, a sonnet divided into an octave and sestet with their subdivisions, or a poem divided into stanzas and subdivisions of stanzas, presents a structural pattern analogous to that of compositions in the plastic arts—and, significantly, Rossetti emphasized that fact when he described a sonnet, in the "Introductory Sonnet," by comparing it to objects of plastic art, a carved monument and an engraved coin. At the same time those divisions and subdivisions within a sonnet or stanzaic poem produce rhythm—the kind of rhythm that can be felt in its most obvious form when one listens to a child chanting the lines of a nursery rhyme or to oneself reading a series of ballad quatrains.

41

And both the architectonic effect and the rhythmic effect can be emphasized or de-emphasized by making syntactical units more congruent or less congruent with lines and larger elements of stanzaic forms. The degree to which Rossetti did this in different poems, his manner of doing it, and the emotional effects that resulted, are the main concern of this chapter.

Actually the architectonic effect and the rhythmic effect are simultaneous and inseparable; and in some verse, rhymed couplets perhaps, it might be impossible to say that one is more important than the other. But in most forms one or the other does tend to be dominant. In a sonnet, in which the internal units such as quatrains and tercets are repeated only once or twice, their rhythmic effect seems slight compared to their effect as elements of a structural pattern, and the same is true in any relatively short poem employing a long stanza that is repeated only a few times—an ode, for example. But as a poem becomes longer so that its stanza is repeated many times, as stanzas become shorter so that their repetitions occur more rapidly, and as lines too become shorter and more uniform in length, the rhythmic effect of these elements becomes more prominent than the structural effect. Most of Rossetti's poems fall into one or the other of these categories—a group whose effect is mainly structural, consisting of the sonnets and various lyrics, and another group whose effect is rhythmic, consisting of the longer narrative and dramatic poems.

STRUCTURE IN SONNETS

In no form of verse is structure more prominent than in sonnets, and in no sonnets is it more prominent than in Rossetti's. Of some 150 that he published (not counting translations), all have the Italian rhyme scheme except one—Sonnet LI ("Love's Song") of "The House of Life," in which the unusual scheme *ababababacacdd* is used to carry the *a* rhyme sound into the sestet for a strong musical effect. All but a few have a pronounced structural division between the octave and sestet, which Rossetti emphasized by having them printed with a break at that point. And most have clearly defined, well-proportioned subdivisions within the octave and sestet.

Rossetti's desire to consistently achieve a pleasing structure may explain why he avoided the English rhyme scheme. Probably he preferred the Italian form's proportions: its main division into an octave and sestet with internal subdivisions seems more subtle and slightly less mechanical than the three quatrains and couplet of the English form. Another reason may have been that the Italian form is more flexible, presenting an attractive structure when divided in various ways. The basis of structure, of course, is congruence between units of subject matter and units of verse as defined by sets of rhyme sounds. But neither Rossetti nor anyone else could always make units of subject matter conform to an ideal structure. "It would not be at all found," he told Hall Caine, "that my best sonnets are always in the mere form that I think best. The question with me is regulated by what I have to say." And he added that "though no one ever took more pleasure in continually using the form I prefer when not interfering with thought, to insist on it would after a certain point be ruin to common sense."[1] He did, then, have a favorite form—undoubtedly the one he used most often, the classic arrangement of an octave divided into quatrains and a sestet divided into tercets. But it was a form that he could not always attain, and it was at such times that the advantage of the Italian scheme—its flexibility—became important. To illustrate: when he had to settle for, say, an octave with its subject matter divided into a quintain and tercet (*abbaa–bba*), the result was still fairly attractive because the two units are linked by the same rhyme sounds running throughout. But in the more rigid English form the same sense arrangement (*ababc–dcd*) would seem botched, because a rhyme sound (*c*) belonging to the second quatrain has been thrust in with the sounds of the first quatrain. In the more adaptable Italian form only the overrunning of the division between the octave and sestet seems as irregular as the overrunning of any of the three main divisions of the English form.

In Rossetti's choice of sestet rhyme schemes the same preference for adaptability to various sense arrangements is apparent, and so are certain interesting traits of his style. The schemes used in the 103 sonnets of "The House of Life" are shown below (those used in the miscellaneous sonnets show no important differences):[2]

1. *Recollections*, p. 248.
2. The exceptional Sonnet LI, with the scheme *acacdd*, I include in the *cdcdee* group. My table disagrees at some points with that of Professor Baum in *The House of Life*, pp. 233–35, which contains several errors.

cddccd: 38 uses (III, VI, VII, VIII, IX, XI, XII, XIII, XVII, XVIII, XX,
    XXI, XXII, XXIV, XXVII, XXX, XXXIV, XXXVIII, XXXIX, XL, XLI,
    XLIV, XLV, XLVI, L, LIII, LIV, LVII, LXII, LXIV, LXXXI, LXXXIII,
    LXXXVIII, XC, XCII, XCVII, XCVIII, CI).
cddcee: 15 uses (XXIII, XXV, XXVI, XXVIII, XXXI, XXXV, XXXVI,
    XLIII, XLVIII, LVIII, LIX, LXI, LXXXIX, XCIII, XCIV).
cdcddc: 12 uses (I, V, XIV, XV, XXIX, LVI, LX, LXV, LXVII, LXX,
    LXXVIII, LXXX).
cdecde: 11 uses (II, X, XXXII, XLII, LXVI, LXXV, LXXVI, LXXXV,
    XCI, XCV, XCVI).
cdcdcd: 9 uses (VIa, XLVII, LXVIII, LXIX, LXXIII, LXXXIV, LXXXVI,
    XCIX, C).
cdcdee: 6 uses (Introductory Sonnet, XXXIII, XXXVII, LI, LXXXII,
    LXXXVII).
ccdeed: 6 uses (IV, XIX, XLIX, LII, LV, LXXIX).
cdeedc: 4 uses (LXXI, LXXII, LXXIV, LXXVII).
cddcdc: 2 uses (XVI, LXIII).

One obvious trait of Rossetti's schemes is their variety—a result
of his belief that "a series such as mine gains rather than loses by
such varieties as do not lessen the only absolute aim—that of
beauty."[3] Another trait worth noting is that all of his schemes suggest a particular symmetrical or proportioned division of subject
matter within the sestet; for example, *cdecde* calls for two tercets,
each having the same rhyme sounds in the same order—a division
that Rossetti attained in eight of eleven sestets employing that
scheme. But other poets—Milton and Wordsworth, for example—
used schemes like *cdeced* and *cddece* that do not suggest any particular sense division; such schemes Rossetti avoided. Since those
schemes cannot conflict with any sense division with which they
are used, they have maximum flexibility—a quality that might be
expected to have recommended them to him. On the other hand,
they cannot reinforce any sense division by an accompanying symmetrical division of rhymes, as *cdecde* reinforces two tercets. Apparently Rossetti wanted the possibility of that reinforcement, even
though he could not always arrange sense so as to take advantage
of it.

As for flexibility, it is an important characteristic of the two
schemes Rossetti favored most, *cddccd* (38 uses) and *cddcee* (15
uses). The first scheme divides well as two tercets, with the first
tercet having the rhyme pattern of a single line followed by a

3. *Recollections*, p. 248.

couplet (*cdd*) and the second tercet inverting that pattern (*ccd*). It is also acceptable when the sense is divided as *cd–dccd*, a couplet followed by an enclosing quatrain (that is, a quatrain in which the separated *d* rhymes enclose the consecutive *c* rhymes as in the *In Memoriam* stanza); or it can be divided as an enclosing quatrain preceding a sense couplet (*cddc–cd*). Rossetti preferred it with tercets, using it only seven times with a quatrain—but in those seven cases its adaptability was certainly convenient. The next most favored scheme, *cddcee*, also has flexibility. It goes best as a quatrain followed by a rhymed couplet (*cddc–ee*), as Rossetti divided nine of fifteen sestets in which he used it; but it will divide pleasingly as two tercets (*cdd–cee*), each tercet having a single line followed by couplet rhyme, with the two single lines being linked by the same rhyme sound.

Surprisingly, Rossetti's preference for those two schemes developed late. He used *cddccd* in only one of the eighteen "House of Life" sonnets written before 1868 and *cddcee* in none. But perhaps because an intensive period of sonnet writing beginning at about that time taught him the merits of the schemes, he used them in well over half of all the sonnets written then and later. The scheme *ccdeed* was also late, but it was infrequent—possibly because it goes best as a couplet followed by a quatrain (*cc–deed*), a sense division that Rossetti did not often use. One scheme, *cdeedc*, he used only in early poems; perhaps he decided that the *c* rhymes are sounded too far apart. The reason why certain other schemes were not especially favored may have been that they contain a sequence of four or more lines in which rhyme sounds alternate, as in the first four lines of *cdcddc*, the last four of *cddcdc*, and throughout *cdcdcd*. Rossetti may have felt that an alternating pattern in the sestet does not blend well with the enclosing patterns of the octave (*abbaabba*).

The favored schemes, on the other hand, do blend well—*cddcee* because it carries part of the octave sequence down into the sestet in the form of an enclosing quatrain (*cddc*) and *cddccd* because it goes even further by carrying down the sequence of the octave's first six lines (or its last six). But in doing this, both schemes violate the prescription of orthodox prosodists, who have traditionally called for contrast rather than similarity between the rhyme patterns of the octave and the sestet. According to a critic of Rossetti's time, the disposition of sestet rhymes "must be such as not to reproduce the disposition of those in the quatrains." Consequently a scheme such as *cdccdc* "is not admissible, because the sequence *dccd* has already been twice repeated in the quatrains."[4] According to this view about three-fourths of the sonnets of "The House of Life" are defective—fifty-three employing one of the two favored schemes and twenty-four more employing one of the other schemes that contain the rhyme sequence of an enclosing quatrain. Rossetti was surely aware of the prohibition against those schemes but he was obviously not concerned about it. His violation of it is one example (others will be shown) of his preference for smoothness and harmoniousness in sonnets rather than contrast—as well as of his lack of regard for orthodox opinions that he happened to disagree with.

A well-proportioned sonnet creates an impression of formality—a pleasing sense of balance, order, and dignity. In his handling of structure Rossetti generally sought that formality. Its primary ingredient, a strong division between octave and sestet, is a trait of 97 of the 103 sonnets of "The House of Life." And most of those go beyond that by adding an attractive subdivision within the octave or the sestet or both. The main sense divisions within the octaves and sestets of those 97 sonnets are shown in the following table:

Octave Arrangements

two quatrains	48
tercet and quintain	9
quintain and tercet	7
couplet and sestet	3
sestet and couplet	2
tercet, couplet, and tercet	3
no main division	25

Sestet Arrangements

two tercets	55
quatrain and couplet	13
couplet and quatrain	8
no main division	21

The combinations of these octave and sestet arrangements in individual sonnets are too various to be described in detail. But the

4. Mark Pattison, *The Sonnets of John Milton* (London, 1883), p. 10.

main types, which include about two-thirds of the poems, are as follows. Six sonnets have a main sense division between the octave and sestet but no main division within either of those units (*abbaabba—cddccd*). Six have a two-quatrain division of the octave but no main division in the sestet (*abba–abba—cddccd*). Fourteen have an octave with no main division and a sestet divided into tercets (*abbaabba—cdd–ccd*). In nine sonnets a tercet in the octave, before or after a quintain, is complemented by tercets in the sestet (*abb–aabba—cdd–ccd* or *abbaa–bba—cdd–ccd*). Twelve have two quatrains in the octave complemented by a quatrain in the sestet, usually preceding a closing couplet (*abba–abba—cddc–ee*). Some orthodox prosodists have disapproved of such a couplet ending,[5] but Rossetti defended it as, though not the finest form, a desirable variation.[6] Finally, in thirty-two sonnets Rossetti attained —more often than any other structure and more consistently than any other English poet—the traditional, highly formal arrangement of an octave divided into quatrains and a sestet divided into tercets (*abba–abba—cdd–ccd*).

The architectonic patterns projected by the arrangements described above Rossetti tended to emphasize, not only by heavy punctuation at the main division points but also by a relative scarcity of punctuated pauses at other points—pauses that would distract from the main structure. As was mentioned earlier, he averages somewhat fewer punctuated pauses within lines of sonnets (6.92 per sonnet) than Milton (7.98) or Keats (7.75). He also uses less line-ending punctuation that does not serve to mark main divisions: 48 per cent of all lines other than lines four, eight, and eleven —the points where main divisions occur most often—are enjambed (Milton, 41 per cent; Keats, 44 per cent), and those that are not enjambed tend to be punctuated lightly. As evidence of his general tendency, thirteen of the thirty-two sonnets divided into two quatrains and two tercets contain no mark heavier than a comma at any point except those division points, and nine others contain only one mark heavier than a comma. All of these traits accentuate the sonnets' structural formality.

However, that formality in "The House of Life" is perhaps di-

---

5. See, for example, Jakob Schipper, *A History of English Versification* (Oxford, 1910), p. 372, and Paull Franklin Baum's criticism of Sidney in *The Principles of English Versification* (Cambridge, Mass., 1922), p. 123.

6. Caine, *Recollections*, p. 250.

minished somewhat by one irregular practice of Rossetti's, and it is
certainly diminished considerably by a second practice. The first is
the use of three rhyme sounds in the octave of twenty-five sonnets
(*abbaacca*). Presumably Rossetti resorted to a third sound because
of difficulty in finding rhyme words; but if he felt any reluctance it
was slight, or he would hardly have done it so often. And he may
even have regarded the trait as desirable for variety. In his defense,
precedents can be cited; one finds three rhyme sounds in octaves
of Sidney, Wordsworth, and others. Moreover, Rossetti mitigated
the irregularity in eight of those sonnets by making the third rhyme
sound, the *c* rhymes, in assonance with the *b* rhymes (*a*:day:may:
a:*a*:face:grace:*a*) or in consonance with them (*a*:red:head:*a*:*a*:
shade:fade:*a*). And he further limited the irregularity by always
introducing the third sound as a variation from the *b* rhymes
(*abbaacca*), never as a variation from the *a* rhymes (*abbacbbc*).
Since the *a* rhymes, running through the octave from beginning to
end, are the backbone of its structure, preserving them prevents
any great structural weakness. On the whole, the loss of formality
caused by Rossetti's use of three rhymes is no more than slight.

But a more serious loss of formality results from Rossetti's second
irregular practice—the slighting of the division between the octave
and sestet in six sonnets by using only a weak pause after line eight
or by enjambing that line in the Miltonic manner. This was mainly
an early trait, frequent in the juvenile sonnets, and only two of the
six poems exhibiting it in "The House of Life" may be as late as
1870. But though Rossetti abandoned the practice, he never expressed disapproval of it, declaring that Milton's sonnets, several
of which have the trait, "are every one of exceptional excellence."[7]
Nor, apparently, did he ever consider excluding such poems from
"The House of Life." From a strictly prosodic point of view there is
reason to feel that he should have done so. For those poems mar
the homogeneousness of the sequence. They stand out from the
others—especially on the page, where they alone appear without a
break after the octave; and their very infrequency makes them
seem all the more like flaws in the formal façade of the sequence.
They are not without structure, of course, but it could be argued
that they are without sonnet structure—that, as one critic says of
similar poems of Wordsworth, "a sonnet in the stricter sense this

7. Ibid., p. 237.

fourteen-line stanza is not."[8] On that view they hardly belong among ninety-seven others that are indeed sonnets in the stricter sense.

Yet every sonnet writer has deviated from orthodox structure, and in English only Sidney and Keats have approached Rossetti's fidelity to it. But Sidney is much more prone than Rossetti to use unconventional octave rhyme schemes; and though he follows a two-quatrain and two-tercet sense arrangement fairly regularly, many of his sonnets are flawed by a division between the octave and the sestet that is weaker rather than stronger than the divisions between quatrains or between tercets. Sidney has also been criticized for sestet rhyme schemes ending in couplet rhyme (*cdcdee*)—a form that Rossetti used too and defended—but his real defect here is that he uses such schemes, not with the quatrain and couplet sense arrangement that they call for, but with a two-tercet arrangement with which they conflict. Keats, in his Italian sonnets, usually has a strong division between the octave and the sestet, and he is as consistent as Rossetti in dividing the octave into two quatrains. But he is much less regular in dividing the sestet into tercets. On the whole, Rossetti's sonnets are the most structurally formal in the language.

What difference does that structural formality make? For one thing it contributes to what Rossetti called "the only absolute aim— that of beauty" by presenting the poems' content of ideas and feelings in a satisfying architectonic shape analogous to that of a classically proportioned building. And it makes another difference. "Romanticism," the critic T. E. Hulme said with some contempt and with considerable justification, "is spilt religion."[9] And many of Rossetti's sonnets are the epitome of romantic feeling—fervent outpourings of love, hope, ecstasy, yearning, despair. Even his meter accentuates that emotionalism by its unusual freedom, its frequent straining away from its iambic base. But religion itself may be either "spilt" as in a camp-meeting orgy or restrained and dignified, with no loss of ardor, by the discipline of a decorous ritual—and the same is true of romantic feeling. In Rossetti's sonnets that restraining factor is their disciplined structure—as it is also in the sonnets and odes of Keats, for example, but as it is not in many of the highly romantic and waywardly structured sonnets of Mrs. Brown-

8. Baum, *Principles of English Versification*, p. 128.
9. "Romanticism and Classicism," *Speculations* (New York, 1924), p. 118.

ing. Unlike her, Rossetti combines with his romantic feeling the sense of form of a classical artist and craftsman; a sonnet of his is not only a vehicle for emotional expression but a carefully shaped object of art. As a result the emotion in his sonnets is not "spilt"; it is confined in all its intensity within a vessel of structured verse.

STRUCTURE AND RHYTHM IN STANZAS

The traits of a stanza can strongly affect the mood of a poem—a fact that caused Rossetti, more often than not, to devise an original stanza which would provide the qualities he wanted for a particular poem. Only a few of his poems, mostly ballads, employ a traditional stanza, and only a few employ a stanza that he had used in another poem. Consequently the kinds of stanzas that appear in his work are too many and too various for them all to be described and categorized. But it is not necessary to do so in order to provide an adequate idea of Rossetti's handling of stanzas. That can be done by, first, describing certain general traits of the various stanzas of the miscellaneous lyrics and, second, examining the particular traits of the stanzas of the longer and more important individual poems.

In the lyrics Rossetti generally emphasized not movement but beauty; instead of short stanzas repeated enough times to produce a prominent rhythm, he used longer ones, from six to ten lines, with an attractiveness of pattern comparable to that of the sonnets. An example is the stanza of "Love's Nocturne," with its two outset lines, its short, inset sixth line, and its elaborate rhyme scheme in which each of the two rhyme sounds is used four times, counting the internal rhyme (implor'd) in the last line:

> Yea, to Love himself is pour'd
> This frail song of hope and fear.
> Thou art Love, of one accord
> With kind Sleep to bring her near,
> Still-eyed, deep-eyed, ah how dear!
> Master, Lord,
> In her name implor'd, O hear!

As for the rhyme schemes, a few stanzas employ consecutive repetitions of the same sound, as in "The Woodspurge" ($aaaa^4$)—a stanza whose unusual shortness accords with the shortness and the succinct cynicism of the poem. A few other stanzas employ a pattern in which rhyme sounds alternate, as in "Love Lily" ($ababcdcd^4$). But most often Rossetti used a scheme based on an enclosing pattern like that of the quatrains of the Italian sonnet. Sometimes he combined this pattern with an alternating pattern, as in "A Little While" ($abbacdc^4d^3$). In several poems he made it dominant throughout, as in "A Young Fir-Wood" ($abbabba^4$) and "The Honeysuckle ($abbacca^4$), in both of which the resemblance to the octave of a sonnet is obvious.

Occasionally a poem's subject matter was such that it gave Rossetti an opportunity to invent a stanza which, besides being structurally attractive, corresponds in an "imitative" or onomatopoeic way with that subject matter. One example is "Sunset Wings":

> To-night this sunset spreads two golden wings
> Cleaving the western sky;
> Winged too with wind it is, and winnowings
> Of birds; as if the day's last hour in rings
> Of strenuous flight must die.

Here the idea of spreading wings is accentuated by the pentameter lines spreading above the trimeter lines, and that pattern is analogous to the poem's theme—soaring hopes and their eventual decline. Another example is "The Stream's Secret":

> What thing unto mine ear
> Wouldst thou convey,—what secret thing,
> O wandering water ever whispering?
> Surely thy speech shall be of her.
> Thou water, O thou whispering wanderer,
> What message dost thou bring?

While the whispering music of the water is suggested by onomatopoeic sound repetition, its wandering flow is represented by the wavering movement, as opposed to a steady rhythm, produced by the stanza arrangement of intermixed trimeter, tetrameter, and pentameter lines; no lines of equal length occur consecutively.

Most of Rossetti's stanzaic verse is narrative, however, and in that verse it is not the structural effect of the stanza pattern but the rhythmic effect of many repetitions of the pattern that predominates. Rossetti emphasized that rhythm by several traits—stanza length, for one. Certainly long stanzas produce rhythm; witness the stately movement of Spenserians in *The Faerie Queene*. But the rhythm is more prominent when stanzas are short, and none of Rossetti's narrative stanzas are longer than six lines, while most have only four or five lines. Within stanzas, the rhythmic progression of successive lines is also more prominent when the lines are short, and none of Rossetti's narrative stanzas employ lines longer than tetrameter. Finally, the rhythm of successive stanzas becomes strongest when each is made a separate unit by heavy punctuation at the end—and Rossetti consistently maintains that stanza integrity. Of his many hundreds of stanzas only ten are enjambed at the end, and all ten occur in only two poems in which the purpose of the enjambment is deliberate. Only ten other stanzas end with a mark as light as a comma. All this does not mean, though, that Rossetti's stanzaic rhythms are unvaryingly regular. They vary strikingly in different poems according to the nature and treatment of the stanzas.

The verse of several of the ballads is based on the quatrain of folk ballads ($x^4a^3x^4a^3$), with its alternation of unrhymed and rhymed lines. Now, any verse in which rhyme sounds occur in an alternating pattern tends to build up a strong forward movement—to the extent that in order to halt that movement poets have commonly shifted to a pattern of consecutive repetitions of one sound at the end of an alternating scheme, as with the couplet endings of the Spenserian, the ottava rima, and the English sonnet. The same insistent forward movement results from the alternation of unrhymed and rhymed lines in the ballad quatrain. This helps to explain the quatrain's impression of an urgent advance toward the next stanza and the next event of the poem—an advance that is faster than that of a common quatrain ($abab^4$) because of the ballad quatrain's shorter second and fourth lines. The quatrain's rhythm is strongest, of course, when all stanzas end with stops and when each second line ends with a firm pause to create a rhythm of successive couplets. That is the usual treatment in folk ballads and in literary ballads too, including Rossetti's. In addition, in the two early ballads "Jan Van Hunks" and "Dennis Shand," Rossetti followed Coleridge's practice of adding a rhythm of frequent half-lines, produced by medial caesuras in the tetrameter lines with an internal rhyme at that point.

But the assertive rhythm of ballad quatrains can become monotonous if continued too long; this creates the problem of varying the movement without totally changing its nature. Rossetti's lively, irregular ballad meter helps to prevent monotony, and in two poems he also made use of another device of variety—the occasional introduction of stanzas that are different from the quatrain but that resemble it enough to fit well into the poem. "Stratton Water" contains three ballad sestets (the quatrain extended by two lines, $x^4a^3x^4a^3x^4a^3$) at intervals among the forty-three quatrains. (Earlier Rossetti had used that sestet throughout "Jan Van Hunks," "In Memory of Algernon G. Stanhope," "The Blessed Damozel," and "The Card Dealer.") In the much longer ballad "The King's Tragedy" he de-emphasized the quatrain rhythm slightly by enjambing about 20 per cent of the couplet-ending second lines and by occasional heavy punctuation within lines. And he again varied the movement with longer stanzas —ballad sestets at a proportion of 19 among the 109 quatrains, together with 47 stanzas having 5 lines:

> I' the Bass Rock fort, by his father's care,
>   Was his childhood's life assured;
> And Henry the subtle Bolingbroke,
> Proud England's King, 'neath the southern yoke
>   His youth for long years immured.

This stanza is admirable as a variation among quatrains. It blends well, being identical with the quatrain through the first three lines. Yet it strongly retards the movement near the end, by its added length, by the shift from an alternating pattern to couplet rhyme in lines three and four, and by the rhyme in line five that, echoing back to the rhyme in line two and enclosing the couplet, seems almost to reverse the progress of the rhythm. Rossetti, however, did not invent either this quintain or the sestet, nor did he originate the idea of using them as variations among ballad quatrains; both can be found among the quatrains of the ballad "Sir Cauline" in Percy's *Reliques,* and both can be found in "The Rime of the Ancient Mariner." The latter poem was probably Rossetti's source (and the former was probably Coleridge's), since he almost certainly borrowed from that poem another trait of "The King's Tragedy."

That trait is the device of retarding the poem's rhythmic advance in especially important passages by using those extra-length stanzas in concentrations. In "The Rime of the Ancient Mariner," sestets and quintains average one stanza in five except in two dramatic passages where they become much more frequent: they comprise six of the thirteen stanzas that describe the horrifying approach of the skeleton ship with Death and Life-in-Death (lines 143–202), and six of the eight stanzas that lead up to the dramatic blessing of the watersnakes (lines 248–87). Rossetti does the same thing. Extra-length stanzas average about one stanza in three in "The King's Tragedy," but they become more frequent in a few important passages. For example, six occur consecutively in a crucial scene in which King James is persuaded to hide from his assassins (sts. cxiv–cxix), and they comprise six of eight stanzas (xliv–li) of a portentous passage in which he hears a prophetess predict his death, and five of six stanzas (cli–clvi) just before he is stabbed. Thus the rapid quatrain movement, varied by those longer stanzas throughout the poem, gives way almost entirely to their slower movement to add weight to the impact of these momentous passages.

The problem of monotony in the stanzaic rhythm of a long poem is exhibited again in "The White Ship"—this time without an adequate solution. Rossetti used a two-line stanza (aa^4) that is essentially a refrain-ballad stanza with the refrain lines omitted from all except the first and last stanzas of the poem and one stanza near the middle. For variety he introduced similar three-line stanzas (aaa^4) at an average of one stanza in five. It is hard to see how he could have done more, but it was not enough. The fault lies in the shortness of the stanzas, which produce a movement that might be called an unfortunate success. It is a success because the steady progression of the lines (all of the same length, all defined by rhyme sounds, and most defined also by end punctuation), and the rhythmic succession of the brief stanzas, do create the feeling of an inexorable advance appropriate to the tragic story of the drowning at sea of the son and daughter of Henry I. But it is unfortunate because that succession of too brief advances and firm halts, repeated well over a hundred times in the long poem, does become monotonous. The poem has been criticized for being too long and detailed,[10] whereas "The King's Tragedy," which is open to the same criticism, seems to have escaped it. Part of the reason is probably the difference in their stanzas; even if those of "The White Ship" are not en-

10. Ford Madox Hueffer, *Rossetti: A Critical Essay on His Art,* pp. 77–78.

tirely to blame for the impression that the action is slow, they do nothing to alleviate that impression, as more lively and varied stanzas like those of "The King's Tragedy" might have done.

In the treatment of ballad stanzas described so far, one sees Rossetti's feeling that a ballad, having its origin in song, ought properly to be given a strong stanzaic rhythm; the poet should use a stanza with obvious rhythmic possibilities and should exploit those possibilities. Most of his other ballads are also strongly rhythmic—especially the refrain ballads, "Sister Helen," "Troy Town," and "Eden Bower." Though the stanzas differ somewhat in each poem, they are basically similar to one another and to their less elaborate prototype in the folk ballad "Edward, Edward." And all three exhibit traits that contribute to a steady, insistent movement: the story lines, three or four per stanza, are all of the same length (tetrameter) and have a single rhyme sound for each stanza, and they are punctuated at the end with remarkable consistency. Only 7 per cent of the 147 lines in "Eden Bower" are enjambed, only 3 per cent of the 56 in "Troy Town," and none of the 147 in "Sister Helen"—in contrast with Rossetti's practice of enjambing more than 40 per cent of all lines in his poetry in general. The resulting rhythm becomes virtually a chant—but not a monotonous chant, thanks mainly to the variety that is continually introduced by the shorter refrain lines.

Those refrain lines, however, may produce one undesirable effect. In ballads as long as these of Rossetti's—much longer than "Edward, Edward"—the many repetitions of identical or nearly identical refrain lines may strike some readers as unnecessary and even absurd. But Evelyn Waugh, after taking account of the possible ludicrous effect of reading the refrains silently, offers a perceptive observation about their proper intention and effect: "Read aloud, these refrains achieve exactly the effect for which they were designed, exercising a hypnotic influence on the hearer, drawing him into the poem, making it hauntingly memorable, and giving it a certain liturgical solemnity."[11]

The rhythmic movement of refrain stanzas could not have been used for the ballad "Rose Mary"; the poem is much too long for refrains and it employs a conventional narrative method rather than

11. *Rossetti: His Life and Works* (London, 1928), p. 157.

the dialogue method to which the refrain form lends itself. On the other hand, anything like the jaunty, aggressive movement of quatrains would have been equally unsuitable because of "Rose Mary's" melancholy, brooding mood. So Rossetti used an original stanza that enabled him to build up a slower but nevertheless powerful rhythmic advance:

> Mary mine that art Mary's Rose,
> Come in to me from the garden-close.
> The sun sinks fast with the rising dew,
> And we marked not how the faint moon grew;
> But the hidden stars are calling you.

The stanza creates a rhythm composed of three main elements. One, of course, is the movement of successive stanzas, which Rossetti emphasized as usual by treating each stanza as a unit; only one of the poem's 166 stanzas ends with a mark as light as a colon. The second element is the rhythmic alternation of couplets and triplets into which each stanza tends to be divided by the rhyme scheme (*aabbb*). About that trait one critic has remarked disparagingly that "if the poet wants his five-line stanza to fracture into two parts each time, this is the structure to use."[12] But that, of course, is exactly what Rossetti does want for rhythmic purposes. In fact he makes sure that as many stanzas as possible fracture by his use of punctuation. The couplet-ending second line usually ends with heavier punctuation than any other line except the last line; in only three stanzas is it enjambed; and in only a few others does it end with a mark lighter than a semicolon. The third rhythmic element is the movement of successive lines; Rossetti emphasized it by limiting enjambment of other lines as well. Only 20 per cent of the lines are enjambed in Part I of the poem, and though this restriction is relaxed a little as the tale's action accelerates in Part II (29.2 per cent) and Part III (32.8 per cent), these averages are well below Rossetti's general average (43.5 per cent of all lines other than the last lines of stanzas, sonnets, and sonnet octaves). Furthermore he rarely allowed these rhythms to be interfered with by heavy interrupting pauses within lines: disregarding exclamation marks used

12. Paul Fussell, Jr., *Poetic Meter and Poetic Form* (New York, 1965), p. 151. But Fussell, while ably discussing the structural traits of stanzas, shows no awareness of their rhythmic effects.

to indicate emotion at comma pauses and colons used instead of commas to introduce dialogue, only three stanzas contain punctuation within a line as heavy as a semicolon. The movement resulting from these emphatic rhythms is not monotonous like that of "The White Ship" because the stanzas are longer, causing less frequent halts, and their rhythms are more complex. But it produces as in that poem a kind of appropriate inexorableness—a feeling of advancing steadily through the tale's ominous events to its final catastrophe.

Rossetti provides respites from that movement, however, by interrupting it at the end of each of the poem's three main sections with the very different kind of verse of the "Beryl Songs." These are portentous utterances of the evil spirits of the divinatory beryl stone against whom Rose Mary contends. Less of a rhythmic effect than a structural effect is produced by the verse pattern, which consists of a single stanzaic form containing some thirty lines of varying lengths that exhibit a virtuoso use of single, double, and triple rhymes, both at the end of lines and within lines. A short passage may give an idea of this structure:

> We whose home is the Beryl,
> Fire-spirits of dread desire,
> Who entered in
> By a secret sin,
> 'Gainst whom all powers that strive with ours are sterile—
> We cry, woe to thee mother.
> What hast thou taught her, the girl thy daughter,
> That she and none other
> Should this dark morrow to her deadly sorrow imperil?

These "Beryl Songs" were generally disapproved of as tour de force anomalies in the poem, to the point where Rossetti himself finally concurred.[13] Yet their complex structure and intricate rhyming do suggest the deviousness of the spirits. Moreover, in the body of the poem the spirits seem too unsubstantial to be dangerous antagonists of Rose Mary because they are only referred to; hearing them actually speak in the "Beryl Songs" makes them seem real and menacing presences.

---

13. *Works,* p. 660, n. to p. 119.

The deliberateness of Rossetti's exploitation of the rhythmic capacity of "Rose Mary's" stanzas becomes apparent when the stanzas of "The Bride's Prelude" are examined. The two poems are similar in some ways. Both are long narratives, set in medieval times, about a woman seduced into an illicit love affair and later betrayed. Both employ a stanza of five lines. But where "Rose Mary" has the adventure and Gothic supernaturalism that caused Rossetti to treat it as a ballad, "The Bride's Prelude" is realistic rather than romantic, concerned less with action than with the emotional ordeal of the heroine—the kind of psychological study that might have been made the subject of a prose tale. So Rossetti narrated it in a conventional style, as opposed to a ballad style with devices such as incremental repetition. And he weakened the stanzaic rhythm in "The Bride's Prelude" to the point that, when compared with the assertive movement of "Rose Mary," it seems relatively proselike.

One immediately apparent rhythmic difference is in the meter of "The Bride's Prelude"; instead of being an anapest-infused ballad meter like that of "Rose Mary," it is conventional iambic. Another difference is in the design of the stanza. Because its first two lines are unequal in length and are not defined by end rhymes, and because it begins like a ballad quatrain but becomes near the end a slower pattern of consecutively rhymed tetrameters, its advance is less even than that of the "Rose Mary" stanza and it does not lend itself to as strong and regular a movement:

> "Sister," said Aloyse, "I had
> A thing to tell thee of
> Long since, and could not. But do thou
> Kneel first in prayer awhile, and bow
> Thine heart, and I will tell thee now.

Furthermore, to a considerable extent Rossetti contravened the stanza's rhythmic possibilities rather than exploiting them. He did not adhere to any regular division within the stanza such as a couplet and triplet (*xx–aaa*); he enjambed twice as many lines (57.3 per cent) as in "Rose Mary"; he introduced a semicolon or heavier pause within one or more lines in almost half of the stanzas. In the example above, one can feel the unsteady, almost unrhythmic progress that results from enjambment and an intralineal stop. Finally— an extreme of irregularity for Rossetti—he enjambed stanzas at the end, seven of them.

In only one other poem did Rossetti treat stanzas so informally and with so little emphasis on their rhythmic movement—"Dante at Verona," a biographical commentary about Dante's life in exile. Here as in "The Bride's Prelude" he apparently felt that the subject matter was not inherently poetic enough to be given an emphatic rhythm. So here again enjambment is frequent (53.9 per cent), no regular division of the six-line stanza (*abbacc⁴*) is maintained, almost half of the stanzas have a semicolon or a full stop within a line, and three stanzas end with enjambment.

If stanzaic rhythm can be given a different quality to suit the mood of different poems, as in the examples above, its quality can also be varied to suit different moods within a particular poem. We have seen touches of this in "The King's Tragedy" where the verse is slowed by a more frequent use of longer stanzas in dramatic passages, and in "Rose Mary" where the verse is accelerated slightly by more frequent enjambment as the action accelerates. We can see it again, along with certain other interesting traits of stanza treatment, in "The Staff and Scrip," "My Sister's Sleep," "Jenny," and "The Blessed Damozel."

For the ballad "The Staff and Scrip" Rossetti again invented a stanza that begins like a ballad quatrain but then changes—in this case by having all lines rhymed and by adding a dimeter fifth line. That brief tail line is peculiarly effective both prosodically and rhetorically. It slows the movement—appropriately for the poem's melancholy subject matter—by rhyming to make a closing couplet and by sharply biting off each stanza as a firmly halted unit. And it makes the sense at the end of each stanza seem like a curt and especially important added thought:[14]

> "Who rules these lands?" the Pilgrim said.
> "Stranger, Queen Blanchelys."
> "And who has thus harried them?" he said.

14. The stanza has been criticized by Albert B. Friedman, *The Ballad Revival* (Chicago, 1961), p. 306, because its tail line forced Rossetti "to contort his sentences and perpetrate ugly inversions." But Rossetti uses no higher proportion of inversions than Tennyson does in "The Lady of Shalott"; some of Rossetti's, such as "fair flew my web for shame," were easily avoidable ("my web flew fair for shame"); and none are more contorted than Tennyson's "the willowy hills and fields among." This is not to excuse Rossetti by accusing Tennyson but to suggest that both poets sought inversions as appropriate archaisms.

> "It was Duke Luke did this:
> God's ban be his!"

The most nearly balanced and most strongly rhythmical sense division of the stanza is into a couplet and tercet (*ab–abb*), as in the stanza above. That is the only division that Rossetti follows at all consistently. But he often departs from it by enjambing the second line, sometimes also adding a strong pause within some line, to produce an irregular, casual effect that diminishes the rhythm:

> For him, the stream had never well'd
> In desert tracts malign
> So sweet; nor had he ever felt
> So faint in the sunshine
> Of Palestine.

What is most important about these irregularly divided stanzas is that they do not occur at random but are confined mostly to certain parts of the poem. This is apparent from the following diagram, in which a hyphen represents an irregularly divided stanza and *r* represents a stanza having a main division at the end of the second line to produce couplet-and-tercet rhythm, with no pauses within lines heavy enough to conflict with that rhythm:

r,r,-,-,-,r,-,-,-,-,r,-,-,r,r,-,-,-,-,r,r,-,-, r,r,r,r,r,r,r,-,r,r,r,r,r,r,r,r, -,-,-,-,-,r,r.

Rossetti has deliberately arranged these regular and irregular stanzas so that they complement the emotion of the subject matter. In the first two of the poem's forty-three stanzas he asserts the regular stanza division. Then contrastingly irregular stanzas and weak rhythm predominate in the remainder of the less emotional first half of the poem, which mainly describes the events preliminary to the main drama. In the second half that drama has begun, with the battle being fought and the queen and her women awaiting its outcome, and it continues for thirteen stanzas until the knight has been brought back and the queen has lamented over his body. As emotion rises in this section, Rossetti accentuates it by a chanting effect, produced by ballad devices of repetition such as a series of question-and-response stanzas. And he emphasizes the chant and its emotional effect by the strong rhythm of almost exclusively regular

stanzas. During the denouement, the last eight stanzas, he introduces four irregular stanzas to weaken the rhythm. Then he uses
two regular stanzas to lend formality to the close. The result of all
this is a skillful and subtle manipulation of verse to enhance the
emotion of the poem.

"My Sister's Sleep" employs a stanza ($abba^4$) that is famous—not
because it was used by Rossetti, who borrowed it from "old English
writers"[15] (Ben Jonson used it, for one), but because it was used by
Tennyson in *In Memoriam*, published shortly after "My Sister's
Sleep." In Rossetti's poem one again finds some stanzas divided irregularly and containing intralineal stops and others divided symmetrically (*ab–ba* or *a–bb–a*) and having no such stops. And again
there is a tendency to favor irregular stanzas in the first part of the
poem and regular stanzas, with a firmer rhythm, in the more dramatic second part. But the tendency, and the resulting difference
between the two parts, is slight—so slight that it is perhaps not deliberate.

Of more importance are two other general traits of Rossetti's
stanza treatment that are exemplified in "My Sister's Sleep." One of
these is his skill in arranging syntax within stanzas in a way that
creates a subtle feeling of proportion and smoothness. This is par-
ticularly apparent in stanzas in which sense is not divided regularly
so as to be congruent with lines and longer subdivisions. Such
stanzas are irregular only in that formal sense, not in the sense of
producing any impression of roughness or disproportion:

> Her little work-table was spread
> With work to finish. For the glare
> Made by her candle, she had care
> To work some distance from the bed.

The arrangement above projects a pleasing symmetrical pattern
which, though very different from the regular two-couplet arrangement, does not so much conflict with it as contrast with it contra-
puntally. One can analyze its symmetry: the punctuation marks are
at the same positions within the second and third lines, the sentence
that precedes the first mark and the clause that follows the second

---

15. *Letters of Dante Gabriel Rosetti*, II, 732n4. Rossetti was anxious to avoid
the suspicion that he had borrowed the stanza from Tennyson.

mark are almost the same in length, and the phrase between the two marks is exactly as long as a line of verse. In another example a different arrangement produces a similar impression of contrapuntal balance:

> Through the small room, with subtle sound
> Of flame, by vents the fireshine drove
> And reddened. In its dim alcove
> The mirror shed a clearness round.

Here the syntactical units separated by punctuation become proportionately longer in an almost mathematical progression of four, six, nine, and thirteen syllables. They thus form a kind of pyramid pattern within the rectangular form of the stanza. In composing arrangements such as these it is unlikely that Rossetti followed a methodical pattern such as can be discerned in them; probably he simply followed his instinctive sense of proportion. In either case the result creates one of the most important general qualities of his style: a pervasive impression not only of balance and smoothness but of underlying control—never an impression of anything fumbling or haphazard.

The second general trait is the special structural symmetry that Rossetti liked to give the conclusion of a poem, a kind of final balance created by the verse. At the least, this usually meant that after using irregularly divided stanzas within the poem he returned to regularly divided stanzas at the close—as we have noticed him doing in the last two stanzas of "The Staff and Scrip." When possible he added extra touches. "My Sister's Sleep" provides an example (and "Jenny" and "The Blessed Damozel" will provide others). In the next to the last stanza, sense is given a more strikingly symmetrical division than in any other stanza of the poem—a single line, a rhymed couplet, and a single line:

> Our mother bowed herself and wept:
> And both my arms fell, and I said,
> "God knows I knew that she was dead."
> And there, all white, my sister slept.

And because those three units refer to the mother, the son, and the sister respectively, the family is united by verse structure even as death separates the sister. In the concluding stanza,

Then kneeling, upon Christmas morn
A little after twelve o'clock,
We said, ere the first quarter struck,
"Christ's blessing on the newly born!"

the balance provided by the main division into two sense couplets
(*ab–ba*) is subtly increased by the correspondence between the first
part of the first line ("Then kneeling, upon") and the first part of
the final line ("Christ's blessing on"), a result of initial spondees
and sound echoes in the participles and prepositions. Slight touches,
perhaps—but enough to make the verse lend an extra stability to
the resolution of the poem.

Rossetti never used heroic couplets, but he wrote three poems in
tetrameter couplets. In the first, a juvenile translation of *Der Arme
Heinrich,* the couplets are handled competently, but Rossetti's ex-
periment with a ballad-style scattering of anapests resulted in a
meter that is too casual to accord with the neat formality of couplet
structure. The second was "Ave," a poem about the Virgin Mary, in
which the verse is satisfactory but not noteworthy. And considering
the dignified, ritual movement that suitable stanzas can give to a religious poem ("The Blessed Damozel" is an example), the faster
movement of continuous couplets was not the best choice for "Ave."
The third poem was "Jenny," which may well be the most accomplished handling of tetrameter couplets in English poetry.

"Jenny" is a 391-line dramatic monologue—or, more exactly, a
reflective soliloquy—in which the speaker, having accompanied a
beautiful prostitute to her room after an evening of dancing, remains
seated in a chair until dawn while she sleeps with her head against
his knee (Rossetti makes the situation intimate but keeps it carefully moral). During this time he expresses his thoughts about her
character and way of life. The poem has been called sentimental,
but that is to miss its point. The speaker does indeed become sentimental at times about "poor Jenny," ruined by man's lust, but at
other times he becomes cruelly contemptuous of her as a tawdry
tart interested only in some man's "person or . . . purse." Thus the
central theme is that conflict between the speaker's sentimentality
and cynicism, which is finally resolved into an unsentimental but
warm human sympathy. And both the speaker's own character and

his varying emotions about Jenny and about his evening with her
are reflected in the artful handling of the verse.

The tetrameter couplet, in the first place, was the ideal choice for
"Jenny." The precision of couplet structure, its simple, obvious ra-
tionality, complements intelligent discourse like that of the poem's
speaker. The tetrameter line lends that discourse more swiftness
and liveliness, in keeping with the slightly racy subject matter, than
would the more dignified and weighty pentameter. And paragraphs
of varying lengths are more natural for discourse than stanzas that
methodically divide sense into units of equal length.

Rossetti makes the most of the form's possibilities, by using a style
that can be described best by comparing it with examples of Keats
and Browning. In "The Eve of Saint Mark" Keats's tetrameter couplets are extremely regular, in keeping with the tranquil subject
matter. He enjambs the end of only about one couplet in seven
(14.2 per cent) and about the same number (16.4 per cent) of the
first lines of couplets. He uses series of as many as twelve and sixteen consecutive closed couplets, and only once does he enjamb the
end of two consecutive couplets. In "The Italian in England" Browning goes to an opposite extreme of irregularity. He enjambs the
end of almost half of his couplets (44.4 per cent) and about the
same number of first lines (43.2 per cent). He never uses a series of
more than four consecutive closed couplets, and he enjambs the end
of series of three, four, and even five consecutive couplets. Rossetti's
verse generally falls between Keats's regularity and Browning's irregularity. He enjambs about the same proportion (43.4 per cent)
of opening lines of couplets (and of the first two lines of the nineteen triplets distributed throughout the poem) as Browning does;
and this, together with occasional stops within lines and a continual
shifting of the position of caesuras, provides plenty of variety. But
he is stricter with the end of couplets and triplets, enjambing fewer
than one-third (30.6 per cent). Consequently, to a greater extent
than Browning he keeps the couplet form established in the reader's
mind as a structural and rhythmic unit. This accentuates by contrast
those passages that become markedly more regular or more irregular than the general style of the poem. And that general style itself
—moderately irregular, easy and flexible, but imbued with an underlying impression of control—is not only pleasing but functional,
since it helps to characterize the speaker as a person of urbaneness
coupled with crisp intelligence.

But when Rossetti departs from that general style of verse, in accord with some change in the speaker's mood, he departs considerably. At times he becomes as regular as Keats, twice using eight consecutive closed couplets, twice nine, and once fifteen. But he also becomes more irregular than Browning, when he enjambs the end of six consecutive couplets. The quality of the verse in such unusual passages, and the way in which it contributes to the speaker's tone, can be shown by a few examples.

One of these is the poem's opening paragraph, which presents the speaker in the room with the prostitute, describes her, and introduces the main theme—the conflict in the speaker's feelings about her:

> Lazy laughing languid Jenny,
> Fond of a kiss and fond of a guinea,
> Whose head upon my knee to-night
> Rests for a while, as if grown light
> With all our dances and the sound
> To which the wild tunes spun you round:
> Fair Jenny mine, the thoughtless queen
> Of kisses which the blush between
> Could hardly make much daintier;
> Whose eyes are as blue skies, whose hair
> Is countless gold incomparable:
> Fresh flower, scarce touched with signs that tell
> Of Love's exuberant hotbed:—Nay,
> Poor flower left torn since yesterday
> Until to-morrow leave you bare;
> Poor handful of bright spring-water
> Flung in the whirlpool's shrieking face;
> Poor shameful Jenny, full of grace
> Thus with your head upon my knee;—
> Whose person or whose purse may be
> The lodestar of your reverie?

The speaker pities Jenny, the "poor flower left torn"; but he also mocks her, and mocks his own sentimentality, not only by the concluding jibe about her venality but also by sarcastic word-play like the double entendre in "flower . . . of Love's . . . hotbed" and the ironic allusion to the Virgin Mary, her absolute antithesis in purity, in "Jenny, full of grace." Even the meter is mockingly ironic in the opening couplet—a falling-meter singsong like a child's rhyme, used to describe a girl who has none of the innocence of a child. As for the treatment of couplet structure, it reflects the speaker's mood by its extreme unorthodoxy: of the nine couplets and one triplet, not only are seven couplets enjambed at the end but a series of five, the fifth through the ninth, have an enjambed closing line following an opening line punctuated at the end—"rhyme-broken" couplets, the opposite of conventional structure. This gives the verse a restless, contradictory quality that accords with the speaker's conflict about Jenny, with his remaining excitement after a lively evening, and with the rebelliousness which, as we learn in a moment, drove him to seek such entertainment in the first place.

In the poem's second paragraph the speaker's tone changes as he describes his normal orderly life of literary work. Here Rossetti shifts to contrastingly regular couplets which reinforce that idea of order and which strongly establish the regular couplet form as the prosodic basis of the poem—while also dispelling any suspicion that the unorthodox treatment in the first paragraph was due to incompetence:

> This room of yours, my Jenny, looks
> A change from mine so full of books,
> Whose serried ranks hold fast, forsooth,
> So many captive hours of youth,—
> The hours they thieve from day and night
> To make one's cherished work come right,
> And leave it wrong for all their theft,
> Even as to-night my work was left:
> Until I vowed that since my brain
> And eyes of dancing seemed so fain,
> My feet should have some dancing too:—
> And thus it was I met with you.
> Well, I suppose 'twas hard to part,
> For here I am. And now, sweetheart,
> You seem too tired to get to bed.

All of the seven couplets are closed and only 20 per cent of the opening lines are enjambed—less than half the average of the poem. Meter also contributes to the impression of orderliness: only 15 per

cent of the feet are irregular as compared with 46 per cent in the
first paragraph. And the one prominent irregularity of the verse, the
full stop within the next to the last line, occurs with nice appropriateness at the point where the speaker's thoughts return to his
present unconventional situation with Jenny. The paragraph ends,
it may be noticed, with the first line of a couplet whose second line
begins the next paragraph—a linking device used several times in
the poem.

Beginning with the third paragraph the verse is given the moderate balance between regularity and irregularity that is maintained
in most of the poem. But in certain passages it again changes toward
one extreme or the other in accordance with changes in the
speaker's emotions. One such manipulation of verse produces a contrast between the first part of a paragraph and the last part. In the
first part, as the speaker contemplates Jenny's beauty and reflects
that a great painter might have immortalized her, that mood of
quiet reflectiveness is enhanced by an orderly passage of five closed
couplets:

> Fair shines the gilded aureole
> In which our highest painters place
> Some living woman's simple face.
> And the stilled features thus descried
> As Jenny's long throat droops aside,—
> The shadows where the cheeks are thin,
> And pure wide curve from ear to chin,—
> With Raffael's, Leonardo's hand
> To show them to men's souls, might stand,
> Whole ages long, the whole world through,
> For preachings of what God can do.

Then it occurs to the speaker that men, far from immortalizing the
prostitute, have contributed to her degradation and lifelong misery,
for which he sees no compensation in a life in the hereafter. As the
paragraph continues, the verse changes dramatically to accord with
this shift in thought and feeling. A couplet is disturbed by an intralineal stop, and then sense rushes over six enjambed lines to produce a brief but powerful irregularity:

> What has man done here? How atone,
> Great God, for this which man has done?

And for the body and soul which by
Man's pitiless doom must now comply
With lifelong hell, what lullaby
Of sweet forgetful second birth
Remains? All dark. No sign on earth
What measure of God's rest endows
The many mansions of his house.

The series of enjambments makes the speaker's words a passion-
ately angry outburst tending to break free of form. But not quite
breaking free—the terse sentence "All dark," contrasting with and
acting like a fulcrum to balance the long, sweeping sentences before
and after it, lends a Rossettian touch of form and control even in
irregularity, like the examples shown earlier in "My Sister's Sleep."

But the quality of anger may vary, and Rossetti varies it in
"Jenny" partly by varying the quality of the verse. This occurs in a
later passage in which the speaker contemptuously denounces lust,
describing it as loathsome as a toad, benighted, cold-hearted, utterly
self-concerned, and ineradicable. These ideas might also have been
made to seem an angry outburst if presented in irregular verse like
that of the preceding example. But instead Rossetti keeps the verse
under tight control by enjambing only one of eight couplets. And he
further emphasizes that feeling of control by making the syntax extremely orderly, using one long periodic sentence divided into a
series of markedly parallel clauses and phrases:

Like a toad within a stone
Seated while Time crumbles on;
Which sits there since the earth was curs'd
For Man's transgression at the first;
Which, living through all centuries,
Not once has seen the sun arise;
Whose life, to its cold circle charmed,
The earth's whole summers have not warmed;
Which always—whitherso the stone
Be flung—sits there, deaf, blind, alone;—
Aye, and shall not be driven out
Till that which shuts him round about
Break at the very Master's stroke,
And the dust thereof vanish as smoke,

And the seed of Man vanish as dust:—
Even so within this world is Lust.

The result is strong feeling not released from verse form but firmly confined within form—an angry but rationally controlled indictment.

As in "My Sister's Sleep," but more elaborately, Rossetti gives the verse at the conclusion of "Jenny" an extra formality and balance so that it seems to do more than merely cease because the subject matter has ended; rather it projects its own impression of conclusiveness by means of a kind of final equipoise. The subject matter ends with the speaker reproaching himself for the mockery he has been using to counteract his tendency to sympathize with Jenny. And he concludes that that sympathy is precious because it lightens the path along which all men must pursue their lives. Then he bids her farewell, not as a prostitute ("Only one kiss") but as a fellow human being:

> And must I mock you to the last,
> Ashamed of my own shame,—aghast
> Because some thought not born amiss
> Rose at a poor fair face like this?
> Well, of such thoughts so much I know:
> In my life, as in hers, they show,
> By a far gleam which I may near,
> A dark path I can strive to clear.
>
> Only one kiss. Good-bye, my dear.

The concluding equipoise comes from several traits. Only six disyllabic words diminish the monosyllabity that lends simplicity and a tone of sincerity to the ideas, and all six occur in balanced pairs: one at each end of the second line ("Ashamed . . . aghast") and of the third line ("Because . . . amiss"), and one at the beginning of each sentence of the final line ("Only. . . . Good-bye. . . ."). Touches of balance are produced semantically by a pair of antonyms near the beginning and at the end of the first line of the final triplet and by another pair, through punning, in the next line:

> By a *far* gleam which I may *near*,
> A *dark* path I can strive to *clear*.

The penultimate paragraph is divided symmetrically into a four-line question and a four-line response, and the final line is divided symmetrically into two three-word, four-syllable sentences. And Rossetti adds a further element of conclusiveness when he neatly solves the problem of bringing continuous couplets to an end by using a triplet whose first two lines make the last couplet of the penultimate paragraph and whose third line, separated, makes a tersely final concluding paragraph.

We have seen Rossetti manipulate the stanzaic verse of various poems to enhance the mood of the poetry—in some cases, indeed, to largely establish that mood. The extent to which he did this seems exceptional among poets, though it is impossible to insist on that point because not enough has been exhibited about the practice of other poets. But for what it is worth, one piece of evidence is at hand. In Browning's "The Italian in England" no manipulations of verse similar to Rossetti's appear; the same staccato, restlessly irregular style is used throughout. Admittedly that style suits the adventurousness and excitement of most of the poem. However, the mood of the poem becomes markedly more subdued in the concluding passage, as the narrator, having finished his tale, speaks quietly and nostalgically of returning sometime to Italy. But the style of Browning's verse is not modified to accord with that change of mood, as it would have been modified, one feels sure, if the poem had been written by Rossetti.

3

Rhyme and Other Sound Echoing

W<small>HEN</small> R<small>OSSETTI</small> read his poetry aloud he was, according to one listener, "the greatest magician of them all. . . . A kind of sustained musical drone or hum, rich and mellow and velvety, with which he used to dwell on and stress and prolong the rhyme words and sound echoes, had a profound effect in stirring the senses and souls of his hearers."[1] A poet who dwelt so lovingly on rhymes and sound echoes while reading would, one might expect, take great pains with those rhymes and echoes when writing, and Rossetti did. One might even expect that he would fill his verse with alliteration and assonance for the utmost melodiousness, but Rossetti did not do this frequently or indiscriminately. He did avoid cacophony, believing, no doubt, that subject matter calling for harsh sound was not appropriate for poetry. And he did usually cultivate an amount of alliteration and assonance sufficient to produce a musical effect. But only occasionally is that effect prominent and the echoing obvious; for the most part it is restrained and subtle.

The most lavish echoing occurs in a few poems in which musicality is plainly a main intention—song poems such as the "Beryl Songs," "Love's Song" in the "Willowwood" sonnets, and "Chimes." Thus "Love's Song" employs a rhyme scheme in which one of the rhyme sounds is used six times (*ababababacacdd*), and it contains triple rhymes, internal rhymes, and heavy alliteration and assonance:

> Alas! the bitter banks in Willowwood,
> With tear-spurge wan, with blood-wort burning red:

<hr>

1. Sir Sidney Colvin, "Famous Voices I Have Heard," as quoted in Doughty, *A Victorian Romantic*, pp. 231–32. Hall Caine describes Rossetti's reading similarly in *Recollections*, p. 217.

Alas! if ever such a pillow could
Steep deep the soul in sleep till she were dead,—
Better all life forget her than this thing,
That Willowwood should hold her wandering!

And "Chimes" is hardly more than an alliterative musical exercise of some fifty lines:

Lost love-labour and lullaby,
And lowly let love lie.

Lost love-morrow and love fellow
And love's life lying low.

In the poetry other than song poems one sometimes comes upon unusually heavy sound repetition used for onomatopoeia, as when *w* sounds imitate the moan of wind in

From *w*inds that *sw*eep the *w*inter-bitten *w*old,

and when hissing sibilants suggest the nature of Lilith, the seductive serpent woman:

. . . for where
Is he not found, O Lilith, whom *sh*ed *sc*ent
And *s*oft-*sh*ed *k*isses and *s*oft *s*leep *sh*all *s*nare?

Apart from the songs and the occasional onomatopoeic effects, Rossetti allows sound repetition to become prominent in one major body of poetry, the sonnets. In fact a few sonnets, perhaps one in fifteen, are slightly marred by expressions chosen more for lush sound than for sense—for example, "limpid lambent waters," "marshalled marvels," and "the pasture gleams and glooms." Usually, though, the echoing is not that extreme but only moderately obvious, and it occurs in only a few lines rather than throughout the poem—lines such as these:

*R*ends shallower *gr*ace with *ru*in void of *ru*th

*Gl*orying I *g*aze and yie*ld* with *gl*ad *g*oodwi*ll*

Like *l*abor *l*aden moonc*l*ouds *f*aint to *f*lee.

Since such lines are often the poems' climactic concluding lines, Rossetti's intention may sometimes have been to accentuate important ideas by heightened sound. But for the most part the echoing is mainly an embellishment—a legitimate purpose, even though some readers might prefer more subtlety. Still, Rossetti's echoing is no heavier than much Elizabethan practice and it is less heavy than is characteristic of Swinburne and Hopkins. Moreover, his restrained use of sound in most other poetry indicates that his relative freedom in sonnets resulted from an aesthetic attitude—his feeling that the sonnet is an elegant genre, a small monument of verbal sculpture for which embellishment by sound echoing, as well as by certain devices of rhyme that will be exhibited, is an organic element rather than merely gratuitous ornamentation.

In the larger part of the poetry—the dramatic monologues, all of the ballads and other narratives, and most of the lyrics—the sound is melodious but muted; one rarely notices obvious echoing. In fact, Rossetti took care to avoid obviousness. For example, he removed the alliteration of "stamped and stormed" from "The King's Tragedy" by substituting "ramped and stormed";[2] and he felt that if "sighs" were used in a line of "Ave," "eyes" would have to be removed from the next line,[3] and that "trembling" was objectionable in "The Blessed Damozel" because of "stepping" in the preceding line.[4] The subdued musicality produced by his characteristic practice is exemplified by "The Blessed Damozel":

> The blessed damozel leaned out
> From the gold bar of Heaven;
> Her eyes were deeper than the depth
> Of waters stilled at even;
> She had three lilies in her hand,
> And the stars in her hair were seven.

Except for the alliteration in "deeper than the depth," which stands out because of the general restraint, repetition that occurs within a single line is subtle—as in the first line, where only one of the three *l*'s begins a word. Most of the repetition is widely spaced, involving sounds running through the stanza in different lines: the

2. *Family-Letters,* II, 381.
3. Ibid., II, 208.
4. Ibid.

l's of the first line echoed in "gold," "stilled," and "lilies"; the short
e's of the first line carried into "heaven," "depth," and "seven"; the
long *e*'s of "leaned," "deeper," "even," "she," and "three"; and the
r's (which Rossetti probably pronounced as a coloring of the preceding vowel) in "bar," "her," "were," "deeper," "waters," and "her,"
and culminating in "sta*r*s in he*r* hai*r* we*r*e seven."

But the echoing does become more prominent in one passage of
"The Blessed Damozel"—the point at which the damozel believes
that an approaching flight of angels is escorting her lover to join
her in heaven:

> The *light* thr*illed* towards her, f*ill'd*
> With angels in strong level f*light*.
> Her eyes prayed, and she sm*il'd*.

The rhyme word "filled" echoes the internal rhyme "thrilled," as
"flight" echoes "light"; and the rhyming consonants of the two former words are combined with the vowel of the two latter in
"smiled." But this heavy repetition occurs at the climax of the poem.
Here, as nearly always, it is only in order to intensify the subject
matter that Rossetti briefly augments the soft melodiousness that
characterizes this class of his poetry.

RHYMES

One of Rossetti's reasons for writing almost exclusively in rhymed
verse was certainly a desire to create pleasing sound. But there
were other reasons. For one thing, rhyme helps to define lines and
stanzas as structural and rhythmic units—an important concern
with him, as the study of his manipulations of those elements has
shown. For another thing, rhyme sounds may be manipulated too,
to produce different tonalities and different emotional effects. And
this was also important to Rossetti; in studying his rhymes one often
finds that traits which may at first seem merely eccentric or even
careless are the result of purposeful manipulations.

Rossetti had a reputation for flouting conventions of rhyming, to
the point that one contemporary critic commented on his "universal
preference for assonance over rhyme."[5] That charge was exagger-
ated; he did not use an excessive number of irregular rhymes in

5. Ibid., I, 435.

most poems. But in a few poems he did use considerably more than most poets would have used, and he did rather often use some uncommonly irregular rhymes. Admittedly some of those rhymes are— or were, before being changed—on the borderline of acceptability or beyond it. Thus *calm:arm* in the translation of the *Vita Nuova* and in early versions of "The Blessed Damozel" was changed after Tennyson called it a "cockney rhyme";[6] and *Jenny:guinea* provoked an objection from Ruskin—which was objected to in turn by William Rossetti as "the stricture of a Scotchman,"[7] and the rhyme was left unchanged. Rossetti himself had doubts about his use of *vault* with diffi*cult,* and though he decided to let it stand, "the distance from rhyme to rhyme being considerable" (six lines),[8] he later changed it to o*ccult* and diffi*cult.* And a few rhymes, products of a lapse of taste when Rossetti was straining for prominent sound in song poems, are outside the pale. Although he himself called Poe's use of *vista:kissed her* "abominable,"[9] it is no worse than his own use of *Willowwood:pillow could* in "Love's Song" or of *riderless: bridleless, fee her:seer,* and *ruin:undoing* in the "Beryl Songs." However, such word-forcing gaucheries are rare exceptions; in almost every other case Rossetti's unconventional rhymes, though they may seem daring, do not seem inept.

The reason why nearly all of those other irregular rhymes succeed is that instead of straining for a correspondence in sound and failing to achieve it, as do the examples above, they seem to deviate deliberately from correspondence, with an effect of stylish casualness. One feels this in Rossetti's use of approximate rhymes—those in which the rhyme vowels are not identical (h*er:fair*) or the consonants are not identical (s*eize:fleece*). Rossetti liked to stretch this license by using rhymes in which neither the vowels nor the consonants are identical (*once:stones, us:rose*). The same freedom appears in his use of light-stress rhymes—words of three or more syllables in which the rhyming final syllable is weak in ordinary pronunciation, used either with a regular rhyme word (wander*ing: sing*) or with another light-stress rhyme (wander*ing:*enlighten*ing*). Rossetti often used light-stress rhymes that are also approximate

6. Ibid., I, 105.
7. William M. Rossetti, *Dante Gabriel Rossetti as Designer and Writer* (London, 1889), p. 143.
8. *Family-Letters,* II, 210.
9. *Letters of Dante Gabriel Rossetti to William Allingham,* ed. George Birkbeck Hill (London, 1897), p. 219.

(*years*:remembranc*ers*, *Eve*:contemplat*ive*, *is*:contrar*ies*). Instead of words having two weak syllables after the stressed syllable, which produce a phyrric at the end of the line, he sometimes used words with three weak syllables after the stressed syllable (*me*:melancholy, *is*:excellenc*ies*), which produce a weak final anapest. And he was fond of light-stress rhymes in which the rhyming syllable is extremely brief (G*od*:peri*od*, t*ell*:audib*le*, h*orse*:warri*ors*). Not that he meant those final syllables to be brief or weak when read, however. He himself, reading with "prolonged . . . tension of the rhyme sounds,"[10] must have given those syllables considerable emphasis, and he must have wanted his readers to do the same. But of course such an artificial pronunciation accentuates even more the unusualness of the rhymes.

Still more striking are Rossetti's ballad-derived, shifted-stress rhymes like spring-wat*er* with h*er*—especially when these occur in poems other than ballads, and even more so when their irregularity of stress is combined with approximation of the rhyme sounds (fl*ees*:dart-rush*es*). They are too infrequent to affect much of the poetry, averaging only about one in three hundred rhymes, but they are too bizarre not to produce something of an audacious fillip. And they were a natural target of imitation, as when Robert Buchanan used them in a parody of Rossetti's style that he included in his essay attacking the morality of Rossetti's poetry:

> When winds do roar, and rains do pour,
> Hard is the life of the sail*or*;
> He scarcely as he reels can tell
> The side-lights from the binna*cle*;
> He looketh on the wild wat*er*, etc.[11]

Although the moral attack infuriated Rossetti, the parody amused him[12]—partly, perhaps, because the imitation is clumsy. Of Buchanan's irregular rhymes (italicized by himself) only the light-stress rhyme binna*cle* is authentically Rossettian. The shifted-stress rhymes sail*or* and wat*er* miss the key to the successful handling of such rhymes. As Rossetti used them, and as they are used in folk

10. Caine, *Recollections*, p. 217.
11. *The Fleshly School of Poetry and Other Phenomena of the Day* (London, 1872), pp. 52–53.
12. *Family-Letters*, I, 299.

ballads, the two-syllable rhyme word ("sailor") is preceded by a one-syllable, stressed modifying word, usually so closely related as to form a compound ("deck-sailor"). Thus the primary stress can be given to the modifying word, allowing the stress on the first syllable of the rhyme word to be reduced, which facilitates some augmentation of stress on the rhyming syllable. This cannot be done with Buchanan's "the sailor," and it cannot be done as easily with "wild water" as it could have been done with more closely related words such as "storm-water." In effect, Rossetti's treatment makes such rhymes not greatly different in pronunciation, however different they are in appearance, from light-stress rhymes.

We may turn now from the peculiarities of Rossetti's rhyme words to the frequency of his use of different kinds of rhymes and the effects he produces by them. The most frequent irregular rhymes in his poetry, as in poetry in general, are approximate rhymes and light-stress rhymes. In his poetry as a whole he uses somewhat fewer of those rhymes (approximate, 4.1 per cent; light-stress, 6.6 per cent) than are averaged by Shelley (approximate, 9 per cent; light-stress, 7 per cent) and by Keats (approximate, 6.3 per cent; light-stress, 9.5 per cent) in representative poems, and somewhat more than are averaged by Tennyson (approximate, 3.4 per cent; light-stress, 2.5 per cent).[13]

But the frequency of those rhymes varies considerably in different poems of Rossetti's:

	Approximate	Light-Stress
	(in percentages)	
"The House of Life"	4.7	10.9
Other Sonnets	4.6	9.4
"The Burden of Nineveh"	7.5	10.5
"The Bride's Prelude"	5.0	6.9

13. Percentages for Shelley are based on *Adonais* and "Julian and Maddalo," for Keats on *Lamia* (Part I) and "The Eve of St. Agnes," for Tennyson on *In Memoriam* (the first 125 stanzas) and "The Two Voices." In counting approximate rhymes I have regarded the established rhyme sound for a set of rhyme words as being that which is repeated by two or more rhyme words and have regarded as approximate rhymes only the words that deviate from that sound (e.g., the third word in *love:dove:prove*). When the set consists of only two words (e.g., *love:prove*) I have regarded the first as establishing a rhyme sound and have called only the second, which deviates from that sound, an approximate rhyme.

"Dante at Verona"	4.7	6.1
"Jenny"	4.3	4.8
"The Stream's Secret"	3.4	4.3
"The White Ship"	3.6	4.6
"The King's Tragedy"	3.9	4.0
"Rose Mary"	1.8	6.4
"The Staff and Scrip"	10.7	2.8
"Sister Helen"	3.3	3.3
"Troy Town"	2.0	0
"Eden Bower"	5.0	0
"Stratton Water"	2.0	0
Shorter Lyrics	5.4	6.8

A large part of the poetry—the dramatic monologues and most of the narratives and miscellaneous lyrics—contains an average amount of those rhymes: from 3 per cent to 5 per cent approximate rhymes and from 4 per cent to 7 per cent light-stress rhymes. Presumably that amount was determined by Rossetti's desire for moderate variety, together with his occasional need to employ an irregular rhyme to fill a rhyme scheme. But in other poems which deviate considerably from that average he seems to have had different purposes related to the special qualities and effects of those rhymes.

One of the most interesting of these poems, because of its flagrantly irregular rhyming, is "The Burden of Nineveh"—an ironic commentary about the glorious past and inglorious present of an Assyrian bull-god in the British Museum, with some jibes about British cultural smugness. Irreverence seems to have been Rossetti's main reason for the unorthodox rhyming—a flouting of rhyme conventions to reinforce the poem's deriding of conventional ideas. The stanza, with its consecutive repetitions of rhyme sounds ($aaaabccccb^4$), produces an effect of persistence that "impresses the steady sarcastic moral," Saintsbury felt.[14] And irregular rhymes add to the sarcasm, beginning with the first rhyme word of the poem, which is both light-stress and approximate:

> In our Museum galleries
> To-day I lingered o'er the prize
> Dead Greece vouchsafes to living eyes,—
> Her Art for ever in fresh wise
> From hour to hour rejoicing me.

14. *A History of English Prosody*, III, 311.

Sighing I turned at last to win
Once more the London dirt and din;
And as I made the swing-door spin
And issued, they were hoisting in
A wingèd beast from Nineveh.

The irregularity continues throughout the poem with a high frequency of approximate rhymes (7.5 per cent) and light-stress
rhymes (10.5 per cent, not counting "Nineveh" at the end of every
stanza—a light-stress and approximate rhyme with the long *e* rhyme
sound at the end of the fifth line of every stanza). More irregularity
is added by one shifted-stress rhyme (rush-wrapp*ing*:th*ing*), by
two cases of identical rhyming (using the same word twice in a
single series, as in n*ow*:pr*ow*:pl*ough*:n*ow*), and by numerous unorthodox "rich" rhymes (having identical consonants before the
rhyme vowel, as in a*new*:k*new*). No stanza is without at least one
irregular rhyme, and several have two in a single series, as in *once*:
s*ons*:st*ones*:z*ones*. Yet none of the rhymes are so absurdly irregular
as to be comic (like some of Byron's in *Don Juan*); rather they produce an impression of cavalier negligence that suits the ironic tone
of the poem.

"The Burden of Nineveh" also employs an interesting manipulation of the rhyme words of the fifth lines of stanzas, all of which
rhyme with one another, using the long *e* as a rhyme sound. In
eleven of the poem's twenty stanzas Rossetti used regular rhymes in
those lines, and for these he restricted himself to five words (and
four sounds): *see, sea, me, be,* and th*ee*. In the remaining nine
stanzas he used light-stress rhymes (languidl*y*, histor*y*, etc.). But
instead of distributing the regular rhymes and light-stress rhymes
at random, he arranged them in a pattern, as the following diagram
of the twenty stanzas shows:

r, ls, ls, r, r, r, r, r, ls, ls, ls, ls, ls, r, r, r, ls, ls, r, r.

Although the pattern is not quite symmetrical (a trait that could
hardly have been perceived in reading the poem), it is obviously
deliberate: after the first stanza one kind of rhyme or the other is
always used at least twice in succession, and five successive stanzas
employ regular rhymes, followed by five that employ light-stress
rhymes. This patterning of rhymes, together with limiting the num-

ber of words used for the regular rhymes, constitutes a bit of virtuosity whose purpose one can only conjecture about. Possibly Rossetti intended it as evidence to counteract any impression that lack
of skill, rather than deliberate unconventionality, was the cause of
the numerous unorthodox rhymes in the poem.

In contrast with "The Burden of Nineveh," certain poems intended to produce a strong musical effect employ fewer than the
average number of approximate and light-stress rhymes. The reason
is plain: musicality depends heavily on rhyme-echoing, and that
echoing is weakened by those rhymes—especially by approximate
rhymes, which deviate from rhyme sound rather than echo it exactly. In "Rose Mary," consequently, in which the rhyme scheme of
consecutive repetitions (*aabbb*) indicates Rossetti's intention of
producing strong echoing, he keeps the number of light-stress
rhymes at no more than the average and reduces the number of approximate rhymes to far fewer than the average (1.8 per cent—an
especially significant figure statistically, because of the large number
of rhyme words, 830, in the poem). In the refrain ballads also, the
number of approximate and light-stress rhymes tends to be less than
the average so as not to diminish the chanting effect. And such
rhymes are restricted to very few or none at all in song poems
such as the "Beryl Songs," "The Song of the Bower," and "A New-
year's Burden."

In still other poems Rossetti chose to use a high proportion of
either approximate rhymes or light-stress rhymes, but not of both—
apparently because of differences he felt in the effects of the
rhymes. Approximate rhymes suggest carelessness by the way in
which they approach the regular rhyme sound while failing to repeat it exactly. In "The Burden of Nineveh," as we have seen, the
subject matter and tone make that carelessness seem like a kind of
deliberate nonchalance about rhyme conventions. Again in "The
Staff and Scrip" Rossetti used a high percentage (10.7 per cent) of
approximate rhymes (but only 2.8 per cent light-stress rhymes).
And in this case the realism of the story and the generally simple
and laconic style make the approximate rhymes suggest artlessness
and sincerity, as if in such a down-to-earth poem perfect regularity
in rhyming would have been an unnatural refinement.

On the other hand, light-stress rhymes seem anything but artless.
Rather there is a suggestion of artifice in the slight prolongation of
the final syllable with which Rossetti must have expected them to

be pronounced in order to bring out the rhyme sound. And the soft languorousness of such a pronunciation acts as an embellishment, he obviously felt; that explains why he used so few of the rhymes in "The Staff and Scrip" and why he plainly cultivated them in the most ornamented of his poetry, the sonnets. The most prominent example of this is the famous "Introductory Sonnet"—a poem which, since its subject matter is a description of the nature of a sonnet, can fairly be regarded as representing stylistically what Rossetti thought a sonnet ought to be. And he adorned it with six light-stress rhymes (monum*ent*, rever*ent*, ori*ent*, etern*ity*, ebon*y*, and retin*ue*). No other sonnet contains that many of the rhymes, but several contain three or four; and the average in all the sonnets (10.9 per cent) is substantially higher than in any of the other poetry except "The Burden of Nineveh."

One other quality of light-stress rhymes seems to have attracted Rossetti. The softened pronunciation of their weak final syllable, as compared to the stressed sound of a regular rhyme, has a diminuendo effect; and he apparently felt that this makes them especially suitable at the end of statements, where they coincide with the somewhat similar terminal intonation that would be given normally. In a few poems, consequently, he made use of this punctuational effect of the rhymes by employing them most frequently where they tend to accentuate the end of one statement and help to separate it from the next—at the end of stanzas and of octaves in sonnets. In a short poem a higher frequency of the rhymes at stanza endings might be due to chance, of course, but not in "Rose Mary," a poem of 166 stanzas in which light-stress rhymes average 3.9 per cent in the first four lines of stanzas but rise to 16.2 per cent in the last lines of stanzas:

Line	Rhyme Scheme	Number of Light-Stress Rhymes
1	a	8
2	a	11
3	b	1
4	b	6
5	b	27

Such a distribution of the rhymes might be attributed to rhyme problems; that is, light-stress rhymes are most frequent at the end of stanzas because at that point particular rhyme sounds have already

been used two times, making it more likely that an irregular rhyme
will be resorted to in order to complete the rhyme pattern. But if
that were the cause, approximate rhymes might also be expected to
be more frequent at the end of stanzas, yet they are not. Furthermore, with a stanza scheme like that of "Dante at Verona"
(*abbacc*), rhyming difficulty should result in no more light-stress
rhymes in the last lines than in lines three and four, where particular sounds are also being used for the second time. But the last lines
of the 85 stanzas contain 15.3 per cent light-stress rhymes, compared
to 4.2 per cent in the other lines:

Line	Rhyme Scheme	Number of Light-Stress Rhymes
1	*a*	4
2	*b*	2
3	*b*	5
4	*a*	4
5	*c*	3
6	*c*	13

In "The House of Life" light-stress rhymes are moderately more
frequent in concluding lines (14.6 per cent) than in other lines
(7.9 per cent) apart from eighth lines; in those eighth lines they
are considerably more frequent (22.3 per cent), thus helping to emphasize the division between the octave and the sestet in more than
one of every five sonnets. In poems other than the sonnets, "Rose
Mary," and "Dante at Verona," this punctuational use of rhymes is
not apparent. The fact that Rossetti did not make a point of using
the device more often shows that he obviously did not regard it as
being of crucial importance. Nevertheless it is an interesting example of the kind of polishing touches he liked to give a poem when
it was convenient to do so.

Rhyme enrichment—that is, the strengthening of rhyme-echoing
—can be accomplished by using rhymes in which more sounds are
identical than in regular rhymes. The most obvious of such rhymes
in common use are feminine rhymes, in which both the stressed
syllables and the following unstressed syllables are identical (*ring-
ing:singing*, *never:forever*). Rossetti sometimes used these prominent rhymes, but he did so with discrimination, restricting them almost entirely to a few poems calling for musical sound. They occur,

for example, in the "Beryl Songs" and in Sonnet LI ("Love's Song"); they are used in a pattern in which they alternate with regular rhymes in "The Song of the Bower"; and they are used exclusively in "Eden Bower" to add a special luxuriance of sound to that sensuous refrain ballad. In other kinds of poetry Rossetti was never guilty of indiscriminately mixing feminine rhymes among regular rhymes throughout a poem, as Keats did, for example, in *Endymion* and as Browning did in a few poems. The nearest he comes to this is his use of two stanzas having feminine rhymes with brief final syllables (*heaven:even:seven* and *weather:feather:together*) among the twenty-two regularly rhymed stanzas of "The Blessed Damozel."

Two other types of enriching rhymes, more subtle than feminine rhymes, are "rich" rhymes, which contain identical consonants before the rhyme vowel (*sorts:consorts, anew:renew*), and "alliterative" rhymes, which also contain identical consonants before the vowel, except that the consonants are within a cluster in one of the words (*roll:control*) or in both words (*plight:slight*). Orthodox prosodists, calling for contrasting sounds preceding the rhyming syllables, have traditionally condemned such rhymes. Nevertheless such a poet as Spenser, among others, used them not merely occasionally and casually but frequently and purposefully as an embellishing enrichment of sound.[15] So also, in certain cases, did Rossetti.

Not that Rossetti disagreed entirely with the conventional objection to those rhymes. He did disapprove of them when the linking identical consonants were too obvious, and for that reason he eliminated such rich rhymes as whisperings:rings[16] and along:long[17] from poems of his own—although he let stand a few others that are at least as obvious, such as *delay:lay* and *still:distill*. However, he usually employed the less obvious alliterative rhymes, in which the linking consonants are somewhat concealed within clusters. And in his poetry in general neither type is unduly frequent; only about one rhyme word in twenty is a rich or alliterative rhyme.

But in certain of the sonnets, perhaps ten in all, he obviously

15. For a discussion of the disapproval of these rhymes by prosodists from George Puttenham to Clement Wood and an exposition of their use by Spenser and others, see Ants Oras, "Intensified Rhyme Links in *The Faerie Queene:* An Aspect of Elizabethan Rhymecraft," *JEGP,* 54 (January 1955), 39–60.

16. *Family-Letters,* II, 216.

17. *Letters to William Allingham,* p. 45.

sought the rhymes. The result is numerous consonant links before the rhyme vowels, some of which are interestingly complex. Sometimes entire two-consonant clusters are linked, with one linking consonant being identical and the other exhibiting only the difference between voicing and unvoicing (*pressed:breast, ground:crowned*). Sometimes both linking consonants are identical, but in such cases the rhyme syllables of the words linked are rarely identical (as they are in *still:distill*); nearly always such links are, more subtly, between words having different rhyme syllables—for example, between an *a* rhyme (*gray*) and a *b* rhyme (*green*) of the octave. Or the linking consonants may be identical, and the rhyme syllables identical also, but the linking consonants may be made less prominent in one of the words by being separated by an unstressed vowel (*place:populace*).

Links involving only one consonant before the rhyme vowel, rather than both consonants of a cluster, are of course more frequent. Rather often words are thus linked both to other words having the same rhyme syllable and to words having a different rhyme syllable. For example, in the sestet of Sonnet LVI the rhyme scheme is *cdcddc* and the rhyme words are *know:screen:glow:unseen:green:snow*. Within the *c* series *know* links with *snow*; within the *d* series *screen* links with *unseen* and with *green*; between the two series *glow* links with *green* and *snow* links with *screen* and with *unseen*. Moreover the rhyme-echoing is further intensified by the occurrence of *n* not only as one of the links just mentioned but also in the first syllable of *unseen* and as the final sound of the three words of the *d* series (*screen:unseen:green*). Other examples of this kind of intricate consonant-linking deserve attention, but before presenting them it will be convenient to call attention to a different device with which they are often combined by Rossetti.

That device is still another method of rhyme enrichment—the use of the same rhyme vowel in different sets of adjoining rhyme words, as, for example, in both the *a* rhymes and the *b* rhymes of an octave. In most poetry Rossetti avoids this practice except in a few special cases which will be described; it is only in sonnets that he employs it frequently. And it is especially in sonnets that prosodists have condemned it. As Leigh Hunt put it, a sonnet's rhymes "must be properly varied and contrasted and must not beat upon the same vowel. . . . It must not say, for instance, *rhyme, tide, abide, crime* . . . but must contrast *i* with *o* or with some other strongly opposed vowel."[18] And Mark Pattison proscribed identity of consonants as well as of vowels and extended the prohibition to cases in which one rhyme is in the octave and the other is in the sestet: "The rimes in the tercets must not be on the same combination of consonants, nor even on the same vowel assonances as those in the quatrains."[19] Against this rule Rossetti is a frequent offender. In "The House of Life" alone, thirty sonnets repeat in a rhyme of the sestet a vowel used in a rhyme of the octave; a dozen use the same vowel for both rhymes of the octave or for two rhymes of the sestet; and one, Sonnet X, uses the same vowel for both rhymes of the octave and then repeats it in the sestet (control: glow: show: whole: goal: throw: know: soul—throat: d: e: note: d: e). And Sonnet LX attains a ringingly strong echoing by intensive repetition (glance: mind: combined: enhance: advance: behind: find: countenance—pain: expand: remain: spanned: hand: rain). Instead of contrasting with one another, as Leigh Hunt enjoined, three of the four rhyme vowels (those of mind, pain, and expand) are similar front vowels. (In American pronunciation the a and d rhymes have the same vowel and all the vowels are front vowels.) And in violation of the stricture expressed by Pattison, n occurs after the rhyme vowel in all rhymes and the nd combination occurs in both the b and d rhymes.

Alliterative rhyming is also present in the examples above (throw and throat, know and note, expand and spanned), but it is even more prominently combined with the vowel repetition in several other poems. For example, in the rhyme words of the octave of Sonnet LIII (grey: face: space: away: sway: place: grace: day) the same vowel is used for both rhymes, and grey links with grace, space links with sway and with place, and away links with sway. In Sonnet LXXX (face: deem: stream: place: race: beam: dream: trace—fullgrown: grey: alone: day: way: overknown) the a rhyme and the d rhyme employ the same vowel; and in the octave deem links with dream, and stream, dream, trace, and race are all linked, while in the sestet fullgrown links with grey. One finds similar repetitions of the rhyme vowel combined with numerous consonant links in the rhymes of Sonnets IV, XLV, LIX, and LXIV, among others. Another poem, Sonnet XVI, does not repeat a rhyme vowel but contains a most intriguing linking of words by means of sounds before

18. *The Book of the Sonnet* (Boston, 1867), I, 15.
19. *The Sonnets of John Milton*, pp. 9–10.

the vowel (*well*: pl*a*ce: gr*a*ce: sp*e*ll: comp*e*l: popul*a*ce: sp*a*ce: favorab*le*—solicit*ous*: l*i*t: *it*: sit th*u*s: s*i*t: to *us*). In the octave *pl*ace links not only with po*pu*lace but also with *s*pell and com*p*el, and *s*pell links with *s*pace. In the sestet Rossetti captures all the sounds of the three *d* rhyme words (*lit, it,* and *sit*) before the rhyme vowel in the *c* word so*li*cit*ous*. And by using *sit* before the *d* word *thus*, and *to* before *us*, he obtains piquant correspondences between soli*citous* and *to us* and between soli*citous* and *sit thus.*

Why Rossetti used these devices to intensify the rhyme sound in some sonnets but not in others is not explained by any differences in their subject matter or tone. However, his liking for a moderate amount of variety in a sonnet sequence accounts for both his occasional use of the devices and for his not making that use habitual. And of course the ideas of some sonnets probably did not permit the employment of such rhymes as easily as did those of other sonnets. Perhaps when he found it convenient to employ a few rhyme words that introduced consonant links or vowel repetition he deliberately sought more, in order to make the intensification prominent for embellishment and variety. In any case, his use of such rhymes is further evidence of tendencies observed earlier: his liking for more ornamentation in sonnets than in other poetry, his preference for a harmonious linking of the divisions of a sonnet rather than the contrast prescribed by prosodists, and his readiness —the readiness of a mature artist confident of his ability—to disregard orthodox tenets that he disagreed with.

Rhyme "coloring" is the use of a concentration of rhymes employing the same vowel or closely similar vowels in order not only to intensify the rhyme-echoing but to endow it with a special emotional quality. A well-known example is Milton's use of eleven rhyme words having the long *o* (bones, cold, etc.) to lend an ominous, mournful tone to his sonnet "On the Late Massacre in Piedmont." Words other than rhymes may be involved in coloring, of course; however, Rossetti used the device mainly with rhymes. Some half dozen of his poems exhibit a concentrated use of particular rhyme vowels to enhance the emotion of the subject matter.

In Sonnet LI, as one example, he emphasized the brooding quality of Love's song by using six rhyme words having the vowels of wo*oed* and Willoww*ood.* And he obviously planned to employ the same soft, brooding tone in a poem about Lancelot and Guinevere (which he never wrote), when he prepared a list of some forty light-stress rhyme words having those same vowels (attitude, widowhood, etc.).[20] The fact that he decided on the poem's emotional tone and the rhyme sounds needed to produce it before beginning to write shows the importance he attached to this quality. In another poem, "Stratton Water," he concentrated rhymes containing a different vowel, the long e of see, for a very different effect —a kind of shrill protest. At the point where the hero finds his mistress surrounded by flood water, drenched and cold, believing herself abandoned by him with her accouchement imminent, and complaining bitterly, Rossetti emphasized the shrillness of her tone by the use of the long e as the rhyme vowel for all the rhymes of five consecutive stanzas (xii–xvi)—although that vowel occurs in the rhymes of only six other stanzas dispersed among the forty-two stanzas of the poem.

In four other narrative poems Rossetti used concentrations of rhymes employing still another vowel—the diphthongized so-called long a as in elate, weigh, prey, etc. His purpose apparently was not to suggest a specific emotion such as melancholy or anger but rather to stimulate a general heightening of excitement to accord with a rise in the action—since all those concentrations occur in passages that narrate the more dramatic events of the poems. Apparently Rossetti felt in the clear, sharp sound of that vowel a kind of clarion quality that accentuates the dramatic feeling in somewhat the same way that a crescendo of trumpet music may accentuate a dramatic moment in the theater.

Consequently he used rhymes having that long a sound in seven of the eight stanzas of "Rose Mary" (ci–cviii) which describe the climactic discovery by the heroine's mother that her daughter has been betrayed by her lover—although in the poem as a whole that vowel occurs in the rhymes of only one stanza in seven. In "The Bride's Prelude" the same vowel is used in the rhymes of only about one stanza in eight except in two dramatic passages: it occurs in five of a series of nine stanzas (lxxxii–xc), the last three of them consecutive, in which the bride makes a crucial confession of her illicit love affair; and it occurs later in five of seven stanzas (clxx–clxxvi) in which she is declaring her shame and anger against her family for having taken her illegitimate child from her.

20. *Dante Gabriel Rossetti: An Analytical List of Manuscripts in the Duke University Library*, ed. Paull Franklin Baum (Durham, 1931), pp. 78–79.

In "Eden Bower" also, a concentration of rhymes having the long *a* as the rhyme vowel enhances a dramatic moment, and here Rossetti interestingly used that device in conjunction with still another manipulation of rhyme sound. Throughout the poem, Lilith is entreating the serpent to lend her his shape so that she may disguise herself in it while tempting Eve. The climax is her exultant description of the anticipated fall of first Eve and then Adam. In that passage the dramatic effect is heightened by the use of the long *a* for the rhymes of five of seven stanzas (xxvi–xxxii). The poem is short enough to be diagrammed in order to show that concentration, with *a* to indicate every stanza of the forty-nine in the poem in which the rhymes have that vowel:

-,-,-,-,-,-,-,-,- -,-,-,*a*,-,-,-,-,-, -,-,-,-,-,-,-,-,-,   xxv

a,-,*a*,-,*a*,*a*,*a*,-,-,-,-,-,-,-,-,-,-,-,-,-,-,*a*,-,-,-,-,-.   xlix

The second device, which accompanies this rhyme vowel concentration, involves the terminal sounds of the rhymes. In most of the poem Rossetti gives Lilith's seductive wheedling of the serpent a languorous purring tone by using rhymes that end with either vowels or continuant consonants, especially *l*, *r*, and the nasals. In order not to interfere with that tone he largely avoids some of the more frequent terminal sounds in English, the consonant stops. No rhymes end with labial stops or velar stops, and only five stanzas employ rhymes that end with the alveolar stops, *t* or *d*. What is significant is that four of those five stanzas occur in a concentration, and it is the same concentration, lacking one stanza, that projects the long *a* as the rhyme vowel:

-,-,-,-,-,-,-,-,- -,-,-,*d*,-,-,-,-,-,-, -,-,-,-,-,-,-,-,-,   xxv

t,-,*d*,-,*t*,*t*,-,-,-,-,-,-,- -,-,-,-,-,-,-, -,-,-,-,-,-,-.   xlix

The rhyme words of those four stanzas are h*ate* it: *ate* it, n*ake*d: ach*èd*, br*avest*: g*avest*, and s*ate* it: *ate* it. While the vowel concentration makes Lilith's voice strident as she gloats about her triumph in the guise of the serpent, the concentration of terminal stops in those words curtails its purring tone and gives it a spiteful spitting quality.

The fourth poem in which Rossetti employs a concentration of rhymes having the long *a* as a rhyme vowel is "The Staff and Scrip." In the following diagram the first of the two symbols used for each stanza (either *a* for a rhyme having the long *a* vowel or a hyphen for a rhyme having some other vowel) represents the twice-sounded *a* rhyme of the stanza scheme (*ababb*) and the second symbol represents the thrice-sounded *b* rhyme:

--,--,--,--, --,--,--,--,--,--,-a,,-a,--,--,a-,   xv

--,--,-a,--, --,a-,a-,--,--, a-,a-,--,--,-a, --,   xxx

-a,-a,-a,-a,--,--, --,--,--,a-,--,a-,--.   xliii

As can be seen, that vowel is avoided in the rhymes of the introductory stanzas, it is used with moderate frequency as the action rises, and it is concentrated in a series of five of six stanzas (xxix–xxxiv) at the climax—the passage in which the queen laments over the body of the knight who died for her. In all of those stanzas the vowel is given extra emphasis by being employed for the thrice-sounded *b* rhymes.

In this poem also, the rhyme intensification is combined with another device. As was shown earlier, Rossetti arranged syntax irregularly in the stanzas of the first part of the poem and thus minimized their rhythmic effect, but he shifted to a regular arrangement, with a strong pause at the end of each stanza's second line and no strong pauses within lines, in order to produce a dramatically emphatic rhythm in the series of stanzas describing the main action. That rhythmic series includes the concentration of stanzas shown above in which rhyme vowel intensification is also employed to heighten the drama. To appreciate these traits fully one needs the contrast provided by the earlier part of the poem. Nevertheless the following passage may give some idea of the effect of both the long *a* rhyme intensification, reinforced by uses of that vowel within some lines, and of the steady rhythmic stanza movement:

> "Uncover ye his f*a*ce," she said.
> "O ch*a*nged in little sp*a*ce!"
> She cried, "O p*a*le that was so red!
> O God, O God of gr*a*ce!
> Cover his f*a*ce."
>
> His sword was broken in his hand
> Where he had kissed the bl*a*de.
> "O soft steel that could not withstand!

O my hard heart unst*a*yed,
That pr*a*yed and pr*a*yed!"

His bloodied banner crossed his mouth
Where he had kissed her n*a*me.
"O east, and west, and north, and south,
Fair flew my web, for sh*a*me,
To guide Death's *a*im!"

The tints were shredded from his shield
Where he had kissed her f*a*ce.
"Oh, of all gifts that I could yield,
Death only keeps its pl*a*ce,
My gift and gr*a*ce!"

This particular kind of rhyme coloring, used not to produce musicality or to arouse a special emotion but simply to dramatize an event, seems to have no precedent. And one is tempted to see it as related to Rossetti's painting, for the painter's trick of dramatizing a part of a picture by an area of emphatic color against a neutral background is obviously analogous to dramatizing a part of a poem by intensifying a particular rhyme sound.

It might be asked, however, in spite of the statistical odds against such a possibility, whether the concentrations just described could have occurred by chance. The answer must be an unqualified no. For one thing, chance would not have singled out a particular vowel and excluded all others, and except for the examples in "Stratton Water" and Sonnet LI, in which a special purpose is manifest, no vowel but the long *a* ever appears in such concentrations. And chance would not have caused those concentrations to occur only in dramatic episodes, never in introductory, transitional, or other relatively unexciting passages. Nor is it possible that Rossetti produced the concentrations unconsciously; he paid attention to rhyme sounds, on one occasion removing a stanza from "Love's Nocturne" partly because he thought it "rather objectionable as resembling in its rhymes the penultimate preceding one."[21] So when he did allow adjacent stanzas to employ the same rhyme sound, he certainly did it knowingly. These concentrations, then, like the various other devices of rhyming exhibited in this chapter, are examples of Rossetti's deliberate, purposeful, and skillful taking of pains.

21. *Family-Letters,* II, 216.

4

"The Blessed Damozel"

THE ROMANTIC theme that made "The Blessed Damozel" extremely popular in the last century—yearning lovers separated by death, combined with the religiosity of a heavenly setting—moves fewer readers today. Yet the poem retains an undeniable appeal. Its form is ingenious, consisting of a description of the damozel in heaven longing for her earthbound lover, which is interrupted occasionally by his parenthetical expressions of longing for her. It is charmingly pictorial, with its heaven like a palace garden where the white-robed elect, most of whom seem to be reunited lovers, stroll and recline beneath trees. Furthermore, "The Blessed Damozel" is one of the most beautifully versified poems in the language.

Both the meter and the stanzas have been much praised. So judicious a critic as Paull Franklin Baum spoke of certain passages as "consummately" handled[1] and as exhibiting a "metrical subtlety" that is "quite astonishing,"[2] and after remarking on the metrical variety of the poem he concluded that "the metre is handled with extraordinary skill."[3] Another critic described the meter admiringly as a "shifting, hesitant rhythm that is practically unique in English verse."[4] Admiration, however, is no substitute for the analysis that the verse deserves but has not received. The only attempt to analyze the meter, by that latter critic, falls short of explaining its unique quality. And no one has fully analyzed the stanza movement or even noted its most important trait—the way in which it is varied to accord with variations in the mood of the poem. In addi-

1. *The Blessed Damozel: The Unpublished Manuscript Texts and Collation,* p. xxviii.
2. Ibid., p. xxx.
3. Ibid., p. xxix.
4. Elizabeth Jackson, "Notes on the Stanza of Rossetti's 'The Blessed Damozel,'" *PMLA,* 58 (Dec., 1943), 1053.

tion, changes were made in different editions to improve the versification, and certain lines, deservedly unchanged in all versions, are striking examples of metrical skill. Some of these have been commented on by Professor Baum and others, but many have received no attention or less than they merit. These matters, then, are the concern of the present chapter: first, the stanza movement and its relation to the subject matter; second, the special traits of the meter; and finally the metrical emendations and other bits of versification that especially exhibit Rossetti's skill.

The stanza is the ballad quatrain extended to make a sestet ($x^4a^3x^4a^3x^4a^3$)—an admirable choice for the poem. Its pattern of alternation, both of unrhymed lines with rhymed lines and of longer lines with shorter lines, produces a steady forward progress, so that not even passages of pure description seem static. And the length of the stanza restrains that progress to a decorous pace that lends dignity to the events in heaven—enhancing especially the "promenade" passage of eight stanzas in which the damozel imagines herself escorting her newly arrived lover about heaven.

Poets who have used the stanza have usually divided the sense symmetrically into three couplets (xa–xa–xa). So did Rossetti; but more frequently than most poets he employed some other, less regular division. And he did this not only for variety but also to reinforce the emotion of the subject matter. The manner in which this reinforcement is carried out is not obvious, but the principle on which it is based is simple: regular or nearly regular three-couplet stanzas are used in the less excited parts of the poem, where they contribute to a feeling of order and calm; irregular stanzas are used in the more emotional and disturbed parts, where they contribute to a feeling of disorder. And in "The Blessed Damozel" the division between calm and disturbed parts can be clearly drawn. Most of the poem describes the appearance, situation, and thoughts of the damozel in heaven—eighteen complete stanzas and parts of two others. In these "heaven" stanzas the mood is relatively calm and the stanzas are relatively regular. The rest of the poem, four complete stanzas and the remainder of the two just mentioned, presents the complaints of the lover or describes earth and its turbulent surroundings as seen from heaven. In these "earth" stanzas the mood is disturbed and the stanzas are irregular.

The poem's two contrasting moods and the contrasting stanza

styles that accompany them are made apparent very early. The opening stanza begins the description of the serenely beautiful damozel in heaven; in structure it is regular, being divided into three couplets:

> The blessed damozel leaned out
> From the gold bar of Heaven;
> Her eyes were deeper than the depth
> Of waters stilled at even;
> She had three lilies in her hand,
> And the stars in her hair were seven.

The next two stanzas are also heaven stanzas which continue the description, and these too have the three-couplet main division.

But in stanza iv, the first earth stanza, the calm mood changes abruptly as the description of the damozel is interrupted by the lover's expression of his tormented longing. And the verse accordingly becomes irregular: the even progression of couplets changes to a restless, uneven movement of syntactical units of various lengths, none of which constitutes a couplet, produced by heavy pauses at the end of lines one and five and within lines three and five:

> (To one, it is ten years of years.
> . . . Yet now, and in this place,
> Surely she leaned o'er me—her hair
> Fell all about my face. . . .
> Nothing: the autumn-fall of leaves.
> The whole year sets apace.)

The effect of this irregular verse in emphasizing the lover's emotion may seem slighter than it actually is. But to appreciate it better one need only arrange approximately the same subject matter into a regular three-couplet stanza and observe how much more placid the emotion becomes:

> (It is ten years of years to one
> Who waits here in this place.
> Surely she now leaned down o'er me,
> Her hair about my face.

Nothing but autumn's fall of leaves
As the whole year sets apace.)

Having now introduced irregularity as the style for disturbed subject matter, Rossetti continues to use it in the five other stanzas that
are entirely or largely earth stanzas. Two are parenthetical
complaint-stanzas of the lover, like stanza iv above. One of these,
stanza xvii, is even more irregular than stanza iv, with enjambment
of the couplet-ending second and fourth lines and with full stops at
the end of the first line and within the third. The other, stanza xi,
is only moderately irregular—a matter that will be returned to presently. The three other earth stanzas contain descriptions of earth
and the disturbed nether universe. One of these, stanza ix, is irregular throughout, with all lines enjambed except line six and with
its two main pauses occurring within lines. The other two, stanzas
vi and x, are especially interesting in that one of them contains two
lines, and the other three lines, that are concerned with the damozel; and the verse is irregular in the part of the stanza concerned
with earth, but regular in the part concerned with her. In stanza vi
the opening reference to the rampart ("it") on which the damozel
stands forms a regular couplet, but when the subject becomes earth
and the lower regions, couplet form is abandoned:

It lies in Heaven, across the flood
Of ether, as a bridge.
Beneath, the tides of day and night
With flame and darkness ridge
The void, as low as where this earth
Spins like a fretful midge.

In stanza x couplet form is disregarded in the description of the
lower worlds in the first part of the stanza. But in the middle of the
stanza the subject matter returns to the damozel, and the concluding description of her voice is shaped into a neatly regular couplet:

The sun was gone now; the curled moon
Was like a little feather
Fluttering far down the gulf; and now
She spoke through the still weather.
Her voice was like the voice the stars
Had when they sang together.

As the case stands, then, all stanzas or parts of stanzas concerned with earth or the earthbound lover are from moderately to extremely irregular. None has a regular three-couplet structure. On the other hand, the heaven stanzas consistently project a contrasting regularity. Eleven of those stanzas (i, ii, iii, v, vii, viii, xiii, xiv, xviii, xix, xxiv) adhere to that regular structure closely, and in the remaining seven the irregularity is relatively slight. In four of these seven the three-couplet structure is prominent even though it is somewhat weakened in one of them, stanza xv, by enjambment of line two (but the pause at that point, between two clauses, is heavy enough to have been punctuated in the 1856 edition), and is somewhat interfered with in the other three, stanzas xii, xvi, and xxii, by one moderately heavy pause within a line of each stanza. Another stanza, xxiii, does depart from the three-couplet structure altogether, but it substitutes a two-tercet main division (for a special purpose that will be shown) which projects a strong enough impression of symmetry so that it is impossible to regard the stanza as being more than slightly irregular. The remaining two, stanzas xx and xxi, seem the most irregular of the heaven stanzas. Both disregard couplet structure in the first part of the stanza by strong enjambment of line two, though they return to that structure with a couplet at the end, and stanza xx has the further irregularity of a stop at the end of line one. Possibly this stanza might be felt to be as irregular as the least irregular earth stanza, xi, which has punctuation at the end of the couplet-ending lines (although the pause after line two is weak, having been unpunctuated in all but the last edition), but which is disturbed by a full stop within line three. However, these two stanzas are at the middle of the stylistic spectrum; and since all other earth stanzas are more irregular than stanza xi and all other heaven stanzas are more regular than stanza xx, the general difference between the two kinds is obviously great enough to affect strongly the emotion of the poem.

Now it may be noticed that all of the heaven stanzas just pointed to as being slightly irregular (xii, xv, xvi, xx, xxi, xxii, and xxiii) occur from about the middle of the poem to the end. Conversely, all of the heaven stanzas in the earlier part are unqualifiedly regular. There is, then, a definite if slight change of style within the heaven stanzas themselves, from strict regularity in the first part of the poem to moderate regularity in the later part. This accomplishes two things. First, it provides the strongest contrast to the irregularity of earth stanzas in that early part where most of them (iv, vi, ix, x, xi) occur. And the one later earth stanza, xvii, is so very irregular as to need no strong contrast.

As a second and more important effect, this stylistic change in the heaven stanzas, like the contrast between heaven stanzas and earth stanzas, is related to the subject matter and mood, and in a very similar way. The subject matter of the earlier heaven passages, consisting simply of description of the damozel and her surroundings, is undeviatingly serene. But near the middle of the poem, in stanza xii, she expresses the wish that her lover might join her; and the next stanza, xiii, begins the passage in which she describes what she imagines they will do when he arrives—their visit to the baptismal well of light (xiii), to the shrine where prayers arrive (xiv), and to the tree of the Holy Ghost (xv), her teaching him the heavenly songs (xvi), and her escorting him first to Mary (xviii–xx) and then to Christ (xxi–xxii) to plead that they be allowed to live and love together as on earth. Then the imagined reunion ends, and in a brief moment of joy followed by disappointment she mistakenly believes that she sees her lover actually arriving (xxiii). During the entire passage one increasingly feels the rising, if decorously restrained, emotion of the damozel—her longing, her anticipated happiness, her trepidation before the throne of Christ, and her brief mistaken joy. And one feels it not only because it is implied in the subject matter but also because it is suggested by the slight disturbance of the verse in more than half of those stanzas. In the same way that the strongly irregular verse of earth stanzas emphasizes the strongly disturbed feelings of the lover, the more subtly irregular verse in these later heaven stanzas emphasizes the more gently rising emotion of the damozel.

The stanzas of "The Blessed Damozel," then, not only exhibit the variety and subtlety that Professor Baum and others feel adds a good deal to the poem, but they also enhance the emotion in a way that adds a good deal more. And two especially striking examples of both variety and emotional enhancement are the last two stanzas of the poem. In stanza xxiii, which differs from the others in employing a two-tercet main division, the first tercet concludes the damozel's imagined reunion with her lover with the words " 'All this is when he comes.' She ceased." The second tercet presents the climax of the poem—the moment when she believes that the angels whose "light thrilled towards her" are escorting her lover to join her.

Rossetti might have put the end of the damozel's imagining at the end of a stanza and the climactic approach of the angels at the beginning of the next stanza. But there are twenty-three breaks between stanzas in the poem; how much more sudden and dramatic that climax seems because it is put in the second tercet of a stanza split exactly in the middle, like no other in the poem:

> She gazed and listened and then said,
> Less sad of speech than mild,—
> "All this is when he comes." She ceased.
> The light thrilled towards her, fill'd
> With angels in strong level flight.
> Her eyes prayed, and she smil'd.

The next and final stanza, xxiv, is unique in combining parenthetical utterances of the lover, used elsewhere as three separate stanzas, together with description of heaven and the damozel. Although these parentheses introduce full stops within the first and last lines, I have not hesitated to regard the stanza as regular in the preceding analysis because not only is it punctuated to make three couplets but also the exactly balanced and parallel parentheses at the beginning and end make it the most prominently symmetrical stanza of the poem:

> (I saw her smile.) But soon their path
> Was vague in distant spheres:
> And then she cast her arms along
> The golden barriers,
> And laid her face between her hands,
> And wept. (I heard her tears.)

As is apparent in this stanza, the poem ends inconclusively, with the lovers still separated and grieving and with no assurance that they will ever be reunited—the kind of "everything to be endured, nothing to be done" ending, to use Matthew Arnold's phrase, that tends to leave the reader unsatisfied. But the structure of this stanza compensates for that. By introducing the device of parentheses associated earlier with the lover, Rossetti has joined him to the damozel prosodically even though the two remain parted actually. And as we have seen him do in "Jenny" and other poems, he has emphasized the feeling of conclusion by employing a more balanced arrangement of verse at the end than in any other part of the poem. Keats, it is worth noting, in a similarly inconclusive poem, "La Belle Dame Sans Merci," achieved a feeling of structural conclusiveness by using a final stanza that is almost a repetition of the opening stanza, thus locking the poem into a circular whole. Somewhat similarly, the extra symmetry of this last stanza of "The Blessed Damozel" creates a final equipoise, so that even though the poem as a story is inconclusive, the poem as a structure feels completed.

As much as to its stanzas, "The Blessed Damozel" owes its rhythmic variety and emotional enhancement to its meter—a meter that is alive but not indecorously lively, forcefully heavy in some places but delicately light in others, a supple, elusive meter with a general movement like a graceful dance. An unusual meter is perforce an irregular meter, and the iambic of "The Blessed Damozel" is varied by a high proportion (30.2 per cent) of irregular feet. That is fewer than Rossetti averages in sonnets (37 per cent), but in the short lines of "The Blessed Damozel" irregular feet become more conspicuous and produce greater irregularity than in pentameter lines. And other poets employing the stanza of "The Blessed Damozel" use still fewer: Wordsworth, for example, uses 21.7 per cent in "The Primrose of the Rock," Hood uses 21 per cent in "The Dream of Eugene Aram" (the first 24 stanzas), and Mrs. Browning uses 20.4 per cent in "The Poet's Vow" (the first 24 six-line stanzas).

But it is the kind and distribution of irregular feet, not simply their number, that establish the nature of a meter. The most frequent kind in "The Blessed Damozel" is spondees, which constitute 14.3 per cent of all feet—an average of three per stanza. Again this is fewer than occur in the sonnets (16.7 per cent) but considerably more than are used in the poems just mentioned by Wordsworth (7.4 per cent), Hood (8.7 per cent), and Mrs. Browning (8.5 per cent), and more than Rossetti himself used in two other lyrics employing the same stanza, "The Card Dealer" (10.6 per cent) and "Algernon Stanhope" (11.4 per cent). This high frequency has led one critic, Elizabeth Jackson, to conclude that "the metrical individuality of 'The Blessed Damozel' comes largely from a tendency to vary the iambic pattern with spondees."[5] Now "The Blessed Damozel's" advantage in spondees over those other poems—an average of

5. Ibid., p. 1056.

one or two per stanza—is enough to account for some, but hardly
for all, of the considerable difference in the meter. Nor does it account for the type of difference. A meter predominantly varied by
spondees would produce a slow, evenly heavy rhythm with none of
the gracefulness, the "shifting, hesitant" movement, that Mrs. Jackson herself feels in the poem.

Consequently, much of the character of the meter must be due to
other kinds of irregular feet. Anapests must be largely discounted
because there are only nine in the poem. Some of them Rossetti
does make very prominent by using the unelidible variety (in seven
cases) and by placing them at the beginning of lines (in four cases).
And these do provide touches of the light, dancelike quality that
needs to be accounted for in "The Blessed Damozel." But they do
this too infrequently to be a major ingredient in the meter.

Inverted feet, or trochees, are a more important factor. Although
such feet are a common substitution in iambic meter, the number
in "The Blessed Damozel" is most uncommon. Where one would expect to find fewer than the percentage in the pentameter lines of
the sonnets (5 per cent), Rossetti uses slightly more—5.5 per cent,
amounting to 28 in 144 lines. The real significance of this becomes
apparent when it is observed that that amount is nearly four times
more than is used by Hood (8 in 144 lines) and ten times more
than is used by Mrs. Browning (3 in 144 lines), and that Wordsworth uses none at all in 54 lines. So liberal a use of these feet in a
kind of verse in which the other poets restrict them to an insignifi-
cant number goes far toward explaining why Rossetti's meter is different. Moreover, the effect of these feet also helps to account for
the special kind of difference that characterizes his meter. Because
in them the normal position of the stressed and unstressed syllables
is reversed, they produce a "shifting" quality; and because they introduce, in conjunction with the iamb that normally follows them,
the choriambic series of a stressed syllable, two unstressed syllables,
and a second stressed syllable, they create a swaying dip-and-rise
movement, as in three of the lines below:

There will I ask of Christ the Lord

Thus much for him and me:—

Only to live as once on earth

With Love,—only to be. . . .

By introducing that movement in an average of more than one line per stanza, usually at the beginning of the line, these feet contribute much to the distinctiveness of the meter.

There remain pyrrhic feet, and surprisingly, considering the general irregularity of the meter, these are only moderately frequent (8.5 per cent, a total of 43, averaging 1.8 per stanza) when compared with the amount used by Hood (6.5 per cent), Mrs. Browning (9 per cent), and Wordsworth (12 per cent). Yet they are extremely important to the quality of Rossetti's meter. That is because of the position in which he uses them. Nearly half (21) occur immediately before a spondee, thus creating an ionic foot (actually two metrical feet) consisting of two unstressed syllables followed by two stressed syllables, as in the first four syllables of

From the / fixed place / of heaven / she saw. . . .

These ionic feet, as was said in the chapter on meter, are not frequent even in pentameter verse, occurring in an average of only about one line in fifteen, and occurring in the prominent first position of only about one line in thirty. In poems employing shorter lines, including almost all of Rossetti's, they are much scarcer. But it appears that he thought of the verse of "The Blessed Damozel" as basically a ballad verse (the stanza itself he probably derived from ballads and he used it in ballads of his own). And in order to capture something of the effect of the ballad meter's scattering of anapests, but without the inappropriate speed that anapests produce, he hit upon the idea of limiting the number of anapests and substituting frequent ionic feet (a device he employed later in one ballad, "Rose Mary"). The reason for doing this is that the ionic foot's two unstressed syllables followed by a stressed syllable produce the quick, skipping effect of an anapest, but the two successive stressed syllables produce a spondaic retarding effect.

As a result, ionic feet occur in "The Blessed Damozel" at an extraordinary average of one in seven lines—more, perhaps, than in any other poem in the language, and far more than are averaged by Mrs. Browning (1 in 24 lines), Hood (none in 144 lines), or Wordsworth (1 in 54 lines). Plainly they are the most unusual trait of the meter and, since they occupy half or two-thirds of the lines in which they occur, they are one of the most prominent traits. They introduce just the kind of shifting variability, the lightness in contrast with weight, the tripping dancelike movement that is characteristic of the meter. Furthermore, they are singularly appropriate to the subject matter with which they are used. Most of them occur in the "heaven" parts of the poem in conjunction with ideas about the beauty of heaven and the blissful activities of its denizens. In connection with such joyous ideas, the rising movement of ionics (and of the occasional anapests) from two unstressed syllables to a peak of stress produces a triumphant leap of feeling, as in the examples below:

> But a / white rose / of Mar/y's gift
>
> Was yel/low like / ripe corn
>
> It was / the ram/part of / God's house
>
> To the / deep wells / of light
>
> With her / five hand/maidens / whose names
>
> And the / dear moth/er will / approve
>
> Who are / just born, / being dead
>
> With an/gels in / strong lev/el flight
>
> And the / souls mount/ing up / to God
>
> Went by / her like / thin flames.

The main traits of the meter, then, consist of a liberal use of spondees, continuously varied and leavened by frequent inverted feet and by the combination of many of those spondees with pyrrhics into a very high proportion of ionic feet.[6]

But so varied a meter cannot be described by a statement; in a real sense it can be described only by itself. Consequently, the examples that follow should provide a fuller idea of how the traits specified above affect the meter. In order also to provide a view of Rossetti at work, these will include the changes he made in different versions of the poem to improve the meter (various other

6. Elizabeth Jackson also notes that ionic feet are frequent but regards them as important mainly in increasing the number of spondees, which she regards as the meter's distinctive trait.

changes were made to improve the sense). In addition, they will include certain other passages that are noteworthy examples of metrical skill.

The opening stanza is an excellent example of the shifting, leaping movement produced by ionic feet, as well as by two anapests, that characterizes much of the poem. At the same time it shows Rossetti changing the merely competent meter of the first four lines of the first version,[7]

> The blessed damsel leaned against
> The silver bar of Heaven.
> Her eyes knew more of rest and shade
> Than a deep water, even,   (1847)

to superlative meter in the final version (lines five and six were the same in all versions):

> The blessed damozel leaned out
> From the gold bar of Heaven;
> Her eyes were deeper than the depth
> Of waters stilled at even;
> She had three lilies in her hand,
> And the stars in her hair were seven.
>   (1870 et seqq.)

Partly Rossetti was improving the sense; but since the damozel's posture in line one and the metal in line two could have been changed without changing the meter (e.g., "The blessed damsel leaned from out / The golden bar of Heaven"), probably much of his purpose, and certainly much of the result, was to improve the mechanically regular meter of those two lines. He did this in line

7. The Morgan Library manuscript written by Rossetti perhaps as late as 1873 but dated 1847 is accepted as a copy of the earliest version by Professor Baum, whose variorum edition is the basis of my present analysis. But J. A. Sanford, in "The Morgan Library Manuscript of Rossetti's 'The Blessed Damozel,'" SP, 35 (1938), 471–86, rejects the manuscript because of some readings which, being identical with those of 1856 and afterwards, seem later than those of 1850 rather than earlier. If Sanford is right, certain 1850 readings that I present as the second version were actually the first version—but the main question, Rossetti's reason for abandoning those readings, remains the same. However, only Baum's view explains why the manuscript contains some patently inferior readings, like the first two lines, that occur in no other version.

one by introducing an ionic foot that represents almost graphically
the manner in which the "dam/ŏzĕl / leáned óut," and by another
ionic foot in line two which lends a metrical and emotional lift to
the splendor of "from thĕ / góld bár." Conversely, in the second
couplet Rossetti wisely smoothed the meter: the removal of one
spondee ("Her eyes / knĕw móre") and one ionic foot ("Thăn ă /
deép wăt/er") make lines three and four almost perfectly regular, to
accord with the calmness (like "waters stilled") of the damozel's
eyes. This regularity gives way to the lifting effect again in line five,
where another ionic foot enhances "Shĕ hăd / thrĕe líl/ies," and in
line six, where two triumphantly rising anapests seem to elevate the
damozel's corona: "Ănd thĕ stárs / ĭn hĕr háir / were seven."

The second stanza contains a purely metrical change which is
further evidence, along with the changes in lines three and four of
the preceding stanza, that Rossetti appreciated the almost onomatopoeic possibilities of regular lines among contrastingly irregular
lines. In 1847 the reference to the damozel's hair contained an ionic
foot:

Ănd hĕr / háir lý/ing down / her back.

But in 1870 the line was smoothed,

Her hair / that lay / along / her back,

to make it, as Dr. Knickerbocker says, "regular to the point of
rippling—an excellent quality for hair."[8]

In stanza v a slight but significant emendation changed an iamb
to a pyrrhic before a spondee, thus producing another ionic foot:

By God / built ŏv/ĕr thát / shéer dépth   (1847)

By God / built ŏv/ĕr thĕ / shéer dépth   (1850 et seqq.)

The final version is more irregular, containing only one iamb, and
where the original line emphasized the particularity of "that" depth,
the ionic foot in the second version emphasizes the sheerness of the
depth.

A change in stanza viii:

8. "Rossetti's 'The Blessed Damozel,'" SP, 29 (1932), 502.

> Till her bos/om's pres/sure must / have made
> The bar she leaned on warm   (1847, 1850)

> Until / her bos/om must / have made
> The bar she leaned on warm (1856 et seqq.)

was "a sacrifice to metrical smoothness," Professor Baum says.[9] But many lines that are less smooth than the one in question were let stand. Mainly Rossetti probably wanted to eliminate "pressure." Its unvoiced plosive and fricative sounds are not pleasing; and its tactile suggestion puts additional emphasis on an idea that is already rather too sensual to be connected with a heavenly maiden—an emphasis that the initial anapest in the first version also increased.

A bit of subtle tinkering is exhibited in the changes in a line of stanza ix:

> . . . Her gaze still strove

> Withín / thát gúlf / to pierce   (1847)

> Ĭn thăt / steep gúlf / to pierce   (1850)

> Withĭn / the gúlf / to pierce   (1856 et seqq.)

Since the first two versions are both more forceful, it is difficult to see why Rossetti changed to the more regular third version. But the first version repeats the metrical pattern of the last half of the preceding line ("Hĕr gáze stíll stróve / Withín thát gúlf") and so does the second version. Perhaps this repetition is what Rossetti decided to eliminate.

Stanza x, included for the first time in the 1856 edition, contains no important changes. But it does contain a metrical touch that is too felicitous to pass by—the use of a dactylic foot (one of only two in the poem) at a point where it creates a tremulous instability of meter that suggests the falling feather that is being described:

> . . . like a little feather

> Flúttĕrĭng / far down / the gulf.

Again some delicate tinkering is apparent in the changes made in a line of stanza xiii:

9. *The Blessed Damozel*, p. xxii.

And we will step down as to a stream   (1847–56)

We will step down as to a stream   (1870)

As unto a stream we will step down   (1881)

In the final version one feels the descent of first the damozel and then her lover in the two dipping choriambic phrases, of which the first is light ("únto ă stream") and the second is heavier ("we will step down"). The next stanza, xiv, contains a line, unchanged in all editions, that is noteworthy for both its perfect regularity and its perfect appropriateness—three end-stopped iambic words whose metronomic beat suggests the pulse-throbbing awe of the lovers as they stand at the holy shrine:

> We two will stand before that shrine
> Ŏccúlt, / wĭthhéld, / ŭntród.

Two puzzling and very similar changes occurred in stanzas xv and xvi. In 1847 the first contained the line

> Is some/times felt / to be,

which Rossetti changed in 1850 to a version that might be pronounced as having an initial inverted foot,

> Sometimes / is felt / to be.

But in 1856 he returned permanently to the first version. And in stanza xvi he wrote in 1847,

> And find / some know/ledge at / each pause,

then gave this line too an initial inverted foot in 1850,

> Finding / some know/ledge at / each pause,

but again returned permanently to the first version. The second version of both lines enlivens the meter; and he could hardly have discarded those readings because of an aversion to initial inverted feet, since more than twenty lines with similar beginnings remain

in the poem. The most plausible guess is that since the subject matter of both stanzas is sedate (the visit to the mystic tree and the
teaching of the holy songs), Rossetti decided to avoid unnecessary
liveliness in their meter.

The most admired passage of the poem is the famous catalogue
of Mary's handmaidens. Their names, according to one critic,
"arouse gliding shadowy ideas of beautiful young maidens . . . a
glamour of faerie, as if one were roaming at ease in a garden of
flowers, where between lilies and roses slender white and rosy
maidens pace to and fro."[10] What is significant is that such a vision
is created by the names alone, without any need for a description of
the maidens themselves—and the names do this only partly by romantic connotations (e.g., roses and lilies in "Rosalys") but very
largely by the sound and meter Rossetti created when he chose
and arranged them:

> "We two," she said, "will seek the groves
> Where the lady Mary is,
> With her five handmaidens, whose names
> Are five sweet symphonies,
> Cecily, Gertrude, Magdalen,
> Margaret and Rosalys.
>
> "Circlewise sit they, with bound locks
> And foreheads garlanded. . . ."

First, Rossetti's emendations: the catalogue stanza remained the
same in all editions, but in the first two lines of the next stanza
changes were made that appear to be related to the catalogue itself.
Before arriving, in 1856, at the final version above, Rossetti had
tried

> They sit in circle, with bound locks
> and brows engarlanded, (1847)

and

> Circle-wise sit they, with bound locks
> And bosoms covered   (1850).

10. Max Nordau, *Degeneration* (New York, 1895), p. 90.

The main purpose of the changes apparently was to employ dactylic words (which need not necessarily be dactylic feet). Such words are infrequent in the poem; apart from the passage above there are only ten, and no stanza contains more than one. But four of the names in the catalogue are dactylic. And the two lines preceding the catalogue contain two dactylic words, "handmaidens" and "symphonies"; these smooth the way for those names by introducing dactylic terms gradually. Similarly, the change in 1850 to the dactylic "circle-wise" and "covered" in the two lines following the names made the termination of that dactylic series less abrupt. "Circle-wise" was satisfactory, but "covered" is awkward as a trisyllable, and the sense of the line is poor (it seems gratuitous to specify that heavenly maidens are modestly dressed). The problem was solved in 1856 by returning to the sense of the first version and employing the dactylic word "garlanded" in place of "engarlanded."

As for the names themselves, in calling them "five sweet symphonies" Rossetti posed a challenge for himself that would have made a failure to achieve musicality all the more ludicrous, had it occurred. But he succeeded, and his success can be appreciated better and explained more easily when his catalogue is compared with a similar catalogue of Swinburne's:

> O daughters of dreams and of stories
>   That life is not wearied of yet,
> Faustine, Fragoletta, Dolores,
>   Felise and Yolande and Juliette. . . .[11]

Compared with Rossetti's ethereal handmaidens, Swinburne's "daughters of dreams" seem coarse. His heavy sound repetition is partly to blame: especially the alliteration of f (probably the least melodious sound in English), the too prominent rhyming on stressed syllables in Frago*letta*:Ju*liette*, and the clang of *and* Yo*lande and*. Rossetti's names also contain numerous echoes—the sibilants in Ce*cily* and Ro*salys* that soften the beginning and end of the series and the approximate rhyme in the weak syllables of those two names (Ce*cily*:Ro*salys*), and the repetitions of *m*, *r*, and *l*. But those sounds murmur; they do not clamor. And Rossetti's three uses

11. "Dedication," *Poems and Ballads, First Series, The Complete Works of Algernon Charles Swinburne,* eds. Edmund Gosse and Thomas J. Wise (New York, 1925), I, 136.

of *g* constitute a fine touch; they introduce subtly just enough hard-
ness to prevent any possible lushness.

Still more of the difference between the two catalogues is due to
meter—while it makes Rossetti's maidens glide and sway, it makes
Swinburne's canter. Inherently, the anapestic meter tends to produce that effect, and instead of mitigating it Swinburne com-
pounded it by making four of his names end with a stressed syllable
that coincides with the metrical stress, thus augmenting the beat so
that it pounds:

> Faustíne, / Fragolet/ta, Dolores,
>
> Felíse / and Yolánde / and Juliétte.

On the other hand, even though iambic is a gentler meter, Rossetti
took care to soften its beat by choosing names that all have falling
rhythm: these begin on a position of metrical stress and by continu-
ing beyond that position they allow the impact of stress to die away,
as it were, in the succeeding weaker syllables:

> Céci/ly, Gér/trude, Mág/dalen,
>
> Márgaret / and Rós/alys.

And of course the terminal pyrrhics in both lines (as well as in the
line just preceding them) soften the rhythm still more. With those
pyrrhics, an initial trochee and dactyl, and only three iambs, the
meter of the names is daringly irregular—yet it blends smoothly
into the iambic movement of the poem.

A final metrical touch: the meter of the concluding stanza is the
most regular of the poem. Rossetti did use, in 1850, " 'mid the poised
spheres," which introduces an ionic foot. But he later rejected this in
favor of "in distant spheres," leaving only one irregular foot (the
terminal pyrrhic in "the golden barriers") in the entire stanza,
whereas the average in all stanzas is six and no other stanza has
fewer than two. As a result, the feeling of conclusiveness that is created by the unusual symmetry of the syntactical arrangement in that
final stanza is increased by its unusually regular meter.

❋   ❋   ❋   ❋   ❋

Rossetti felt that he had more thoroughly "mastered the means"
of presenting artistic conceptions in poetry than in painting, but he
never explained what he meant by "means." In a sense this study

has been an attempt to find out. The result has been to exhibit numerous traits of his verse structure, meter, and sound—too many to be recapitulated here. But some observations can be made about what those traits imply.

Most obviously they show a craftsman's concern for achieving just the right versification down to the least detail, as in the changes made in "The Blessed Damozel" over more than twenty years to polish verse that was excellent in the beginning. This is ample evidence to verify his brother's opinion that Rossetti was "a very fastidious writer" and his own remark that poetry was the art in which he had done "no pot-boiling" and which he had not "treated shabbily."[12] Such care was due not to a temperamental meticulousness (Rossetti could be most careless about matters other than art) but to his feeling that a poem is more than a means of expression—that it is pre-eminently an object of art.

This relates to the question of what effect Rossetti's painting had on his poetry. His colorful poetic imagery, it is often said, reveals the painter. Yet even a poem as colorful as "The Blessed Damozel" is no more so than, say, Keats's "The Eve of St. Agnes" or Tennyson's "The Lady of Shalott." A more valid connection can be found in structure. Rossetti tends to base entire poems on a single static scene—a paintable scene, that is—which presents persons whose thoughts or speeches constitute the poem. "The Blessed Damozel," "Jenny," "The Bride's Prelude," and various sonnets are examples. And he sometimes painted those scenes or, conversely, wrote poems based on scenes he or someone else had painted.

Rossetti's versification, however, may have an even more important, if less demonstrable, connection with his painting. A painting must be more than an idea illustrated; it must be an object of beauty. It can be made so only by a mastery of technique and care in employing it. Poetry, on the other hand, may seem to require only poetic ideas, with little more technique than the verbal skill many people develop, exerted to the extent of producing acceptable rhythm and sound. Rossetti went beyond that notion—unlike some who became poets of distinction in most respects but remained only amateurs in prosody when compared with craftsmen like Spenser, Milton, and Pope. It seems probable that Rossetti's experience in painting influenced him to regard poetry similarly as an art in which good craftsmanship is invaluable, and to perceive

12. *Letters of Dante Gabriel Rossetti*, II, 729.

that, like subtle nuances of color, line, and composition, subtle nuances of sound, rhythm, and structure may greatly enhance emotion.

As for other influences, Rossetti, who studied Shelley's versification at fifteen, must have learned things from much of what he read, and he read a great deal. More specifically, folk ballads and probably Coleridge influenced the stanzas, meter, and rhymes of his own ballads. The formality of his sonnet structure undoubtedly owes something to the Italian sonnet writers he translated. Shelley may have influenced his sometimes lavish use of approximate rhymes, Spenser his concentrations of alliterative rhymes in some sonnets, and Milton his concentrations of different rhymes employing the same vowel. But many of his special practices do not occur, or have not been pointed out, in other poets.

For Rossetti was independent, original, and inventive—independent in disregarding orthodox rules he disagreed with, original even in reviving and adapting the folk ballad meter and refrain stanza instead of simply writing as his contemporaries wrote, and both original and inventive in devising his own techniques. One of many indications of this is his development of no fewer than five different meters within the iambic tradition alone—the subtly distinctive sonnet meter, the anapest-sprinkled folk imitation of certain ballads, the irregular trimeter of a few lyrics that anticipated the loose iambic of Yeats and others, and the unique meters of "Rose Mary" and "The Blessed Damozel"—plus the excitingly varied trochaic of "Eden Bower." Another indication is his devising of stanzas to produce the right movement for particular poems, and his manipulation of those stanzaic rhythms, to an extent for which no precedent is apparent, according to the mood of different poems and passages within poems.

How many of the traits of rhythm and sound that we have seen thus operating in the poetry were deliberate? The question is not relevant to their effect on the reader but it is relevant to our understanding of how the poet worked. Practically all of them, one feels safe in answering. When one observes in "Rose Mary" and "The Bride's Prelude," for example, a difference in stanza treatment so consistent that it could only be deliberate, one is convinced that similar though more subtle differences in other poems must also be deliberate. And when one notes in Rossetti's letters his frequent worrying about the sound or meter of even a single word in a long poem, one feels sure that little in any of the poems is accidental.

And how important are those prosodic traits to the poetry? Plainly Rossetti, who labored to produce them, thought they were essential. And in this study, by pointing to their effects and in some cases illustrating those effects by comparisons, I have tried to show that he was right—that the various devices he employed are indispensable to the emotion of his poems. What is more, they are contributions to the technical resources of English prosody.

UNIVERSITY OF FLORIDA MONOGRAPHS

Humanities

No. 1: *Uncollected Letters of James Gates Percival,* edited by Harry R. Warfel

No. 2: *Leigh Hunt's Autobiography: The Earliest Sketches,* edited by Stephen F. Fogle

No. 3: *Pause Patterns in Elizabethan and Jacobean Drama,* by Ants Oras

No. 4: *Rhetoric and American Poetry of the Early National Period,* by Gordon E. Bigelow

No. 5: *The Background of* The Princess Casamassima, by W. H. Tilley

No. 6: *Indian Sculpture in the John and Mable Ringling Museum of Art,* by Roy C. Craven, Jr.

No. 7: *The Cestus. A Mask,* edited by Thomas B. Stroup

No. 8: Tamburlaine, Part I, *and Its Audience,* by Frank B. Fieler

No. 9: *The Case of John Darrell: Minister and Exorcist,* by Corinne Holt Rickert

No. 10: *Reflections of the Civil War in Southern Humor,* by Wade H. Hall

No. 11: *Charles Dodgson, Semeiotician,* by Daniel F. Kirk

No. 12: *Three Middle English Religious Poems,* edited by R. H. Bowers

No. 13: *The Existentialism of Miguel de Unamuno,* by José Huertas-Jourda

No. 14: *Four Spiritual Crises in Mid-Century American Fiction,* by Robert Detweiler

No. 15: *Style and Society in German Literary Expressionism,* by Egbert Krispyn

No. 16: *The Reach of Art: A Study in the Prosody of Pope,* by Jacob H. Adler

No. 17: *Malraux, Sartre, and Aragon as Political Novelists,* by Catharine Savage

No. 18: *Las Guerras Carlistas y el Reinado Isabelino en la Obra de Ramón del Valle-Inclán,* por María Dolores Lado

No. 19: *Diderot's* Vie de Sénèque: *A Swan Song Revised,* by Douglas A. Bonneville

No. 20: *Blank Verse and Chronology in Milton,* by Ants Oras

No. 21: *Milton's Elisions,* by Robert O. Evans

No. 22: *Prayer in Sixteenth-Century England,* by Faye L. Kelly

No. 23: *The Strangers: The Tragic World of Tristan L'Hermite,* by Claude K. Abraham

No. 24: *Dramatic Uses of Biblical Allusion in Marlowe and Shakespeare,* by James H. Sims

No. 25: *Doubt and Dogma in Maria Edgeworth,* by Mark D. Hawthorne

No. 26: *The Masses of Francesco Soriano,* by S. Philip Kniseley

No. 27: *Love as Death in* The Iceman Cometh, by Winifred Dusenbury Frazer

No. 28: *Melville and Authority,* by Nicholas Canaday, Jr.

No. 29: *Don Quixote: Hero or Fool? A Study in Narrative Technique,* by John J. Allen

No. 30: *Ideal and Reality in the Fictional Narratives of Théophile Gautier,* by Albert B. Smith

No. 31: *Negritude as a Theme in the Poetry of the Portuguese-Speaking World,* by Richard A. Preto-Rodas

No. 32: *The Criticism of Photography as Art: The Photographs of Jerry Uelsmann,* by John L. Ward

No. 33: *The Kingdom of God in the Synoptic Tradition,* by Richard H. Hiers

No. 34: *Dante Gabriel Rossetti's Versecraft,* by Joseph F. Vogel